CONNECT WITH YOUR

INNER CALM

Shift from FEAR to LOVE through the power of
energy, clarity, and connection

Jenna Bambe

DEDICATION

With profound gratitude, I dedicate this book to

Joseph Carbone, my spiritual guide and mentor.
Your teachings have been the cornerstone of my
understanding—shaping not only the words
within these pages but the very essence of who I
am. Your wisdom and presence have
illuminated my path, and I remain in awe of the
depth and grace you've brought to my journey.

With heartfelt appreciation,

Jenna Bambe

ACKNOWLEDGMENT

To my two beautiful daughters, Katie and Emma—your kindness, authenticity, and strength make me endlessly proud. Your love and patience sustained me through this writing journey, and your unwavering support is my greatest blessing.

To those whose search for truth rekindled my own faith in what's possible—thank you for walking the path beside me.

ABOUT THIS BOOK

Guiding information and practices to help you reconnect with yourself, shift your energy, and live in alignment with your truth.

Each chapter includes a *Practice With Me* session– simple tools and intuitive guidance to help you shift your state, raise your vibrational frequency, and help you return to your inner calm.

Table of Contents

Part One

Foundations

Chapter 1

Know Your Dream

The heart of this book is an invitation.

It is an invitation to align with your soul—to feel calm, connected, and at home within yourself.

From that space, you can begin to see your life with new awareness—and feel more empowered and steady as you move through it.

Your path doesn't need fixing.

It's a gateway.

A way to create a daily practice that supports you—emotionally, spiritually, and physically.

You'll be guided to build that practice not through perfection, but through presence. Even when fear or doubt arises, you'll learn how to return to yourself with grace.

This is how you reconnect with your inner calm.

This is how transformation begins — quietly and steadily, and then all at once you realize you're living with more peace and purpose than you ever imagined.

This book unfolds in gentle layers, offering teachings and tools to help you reconnect with yourself and align with your soul's path.

You'll be introduced to gentle practices that combine spiritual tools with their own unique gifts —all designed to help you stay rooted in the sanctuary within.

Here's what you can expect as you journey through the chapters ahead:

✦ We begin with **desire**—not as something to suppress, but as something sacred. A spark from the soul, asking you to expand, align, and create from love.

✦ Next, we explore **daily tools and rituals** that help you return to clarity and release what no longer serves. These practices create space for peace and self-trust.

✦   From there, you'll learn how to **create consciously**, aligning your thoughts and actions with the values and intentions that reflect your soul.

✦   Then, we move into **deeper connection with your intuition**— remembering that you already carry the wisdom and sensitivity you need to live from your truth.

✦   Finally, we'll explore what it means to **honor your process**: the slow unfolding, the imperfect steps, the daily choices that bring you back to your center.

✦   From this grounded space, you begin to live a soul-sustained life; one filled with joy and a lasting connection to your sacred self.

Each chapter includes soul guidance, energy teachings, and *Practice With Me* sessions to help you gently apply what you're learning.

Let them meet you softly. Skip them or return to them as you need. There's no pressure here. Just a quiet space to reflect, reconnect, and gently remember your own inner truth.

You don't need to be perfect.

You don't need to rush.

You only need to begin—and keep choosing to return.

How This Practice Changed My Life

Over thirty years ago, I was searching for something deeper. I longed for peace and meaning, but I didn't know where to find it. Then I met a spiritual teacher—an energy healer who had devoted his retirement to connecting with God and helping others. He became my mentor, and the practices he taught me became the foundation of everything I now share.

He showed me how to receive energy and healing, release subconscious negativity, and return to inner calm. I could feel myself beginning to align with a higher frequency of love, clarity, and peace.

As I used my practice, I began to heal. My anxiety began to heal and even a stomach ulcer cleared. I found the strength to leave a damaging relationship and began trusting my intuition for the first time in my life. That trust changed everything.

But the true beginning of my story, on a soul level, started when I was six years old. At the time, I was living in Scotland when I suddenly became completely deaf. It was a lonely and isolating experience. After several months and many visits to different doctors, it was finally confirmed that I needed surgery to restore my hearing.

During the surgery, I had an out-of-body experience. I floated above the table and watched the surgery from the ceiling Then I rose even higher and was met by a being of pure love. In that moment, I knew it was God.

I was told I had a choice: I could stay, or I could return to my body and live this life. I remember being told that this life held value—both for what I would learn, and for what I could give. The love I felt in that moment was overwhelming, like coming home. It was everything I've been striving to create ever since: so much peace, so much belonging.

I chose to return—not because I wanted to, but because I wanted to honor that love. When I awoke from surgery, it was a relief to hear again. I remember asking everyone why they were shouting. But what stayed with me most was not the sound—it was the intense love I had felt during that experience.

The next day, I sat by a window in the children's ward, looking out at a grassy area with greenhouses in the distance. I remember longing to relive that sacred moment. Even now, the sight of a greenhouse brings me back to it.

You don't need to have a near death experience to come close to this kind of peace. Every one of us experiences moments—often small and quiet — that feel mysterious and deeply alive.

When you revisit those memories, you can experience wonder and strength. From that place, you may feel more open to possibilities you hadn't seen before, and from there, you can create what you truly want.

Years later, that memory stayed alive inside of me. I was 23 when I felt a quiet urgency to align more deeply with God. That early glimpse of love was calling me forward, asking me to remember who I was and to begin making changes.

I was in nursing school when my boyfriend proposed. Soon after, everything shifted. He was taking steroids for a recently diagnoses autoimmune disease, and his moods grew unstable—rages, threats, demands. He pressured me to ask my father for money to buy a mansion, something far beyond what we needed or could afford. When I said no, his anger only escalated.

Then strange things began to happen. He started waking in the night claiming to see male spirits sitting around me It's "them or us," he said. "I can't handle it anymore."

I wanted to rationalize it, to blame the medication he was taking, but deep down, I knew something wasn't right. I needed help.

I reached out to a friend of my father's—a former social worker, who after her husband's passing, had become a medium. She understood immediately. I wasn't seeking contact with ghosts—I was looking for something steadier, something closer to God— an explanation for what my fiancé was seeing. She referred me to a spiritual mentor named Joseph.

Joseph had retired from the corporate world and devoted his life to healing. He introduced me to everything I now know. Today, at 103 years old, he still does energy work to help raise global awareness.

Through him, I came to understand that the spirits my fiancé saw weren't meant to frighten me—they were warning me, showing me the path I was meant to take. They helped me recognize I was being guided toward something higher— and reminded me that no one else can do our inner work for us. *Each of us must be the guardian of our own soul.*

Everyone moves through difficult seasons. During these times, it can feel like the ground has shifted under our feet. It's times we can feel powerless, but the truth is different.

Each difficult season is an invitation to choose— will we collapse in fear, or turn toward our soul self and inner truth? When we stay open and align with that truth, we step into possibilities we may not have even realized were there before.

Years later, as a hospice nurse, I began walking beside people at the end of life. I worked with patients and families to help them access peace, and release fear.

Even before my hospice work, I had received subtle messages from souls who had passed— usually loved ones of friends. Their presence was gentle, many times overjoyed, and most often offering comfort and reassurance to those still living.

If you've ever lost someone dear to you, you may have already felt flickers of their presence— a scent, a dream, a sudden sense of warmth or comfort. These quiet moments are reminders that the connection with those we cherish can continue on in ways we may not fully understand.

With a gentle open awareness, you can begin to sense your loved one's energy— often in ways that feel subtle and very natural. What matters is not the "how" but the peace it can bring—

especially for those who need to feel that unseen love and connection.

As we learn to trust our connection to those sacred moments, it becomes clear that true healing comes from remembering who we really are.

Healing doesn't come from chasing outcomes; it arises from the calm beneath the storm, the soul beneath the fear.

Healing is accepting ourselves. It's trusting our worth.

It's where we stop grasping. We begin giving freely.

From that place of generosity and surrender, the universe responds. That's what this book is about, not performance, but practice.

✦ Practice With Me: A Moment of Soul Memory

Find a quiet space where you won't be interrupted. Place your hand gently on your heart and let your breath slow.

As you breathe, allow yourself to soften into these reflections.

Soul Memory

Think back to a moment that felt mysterious, spiritual, or deeply peaceful—whether as a child, or any other time in your life.

✦   What do you remember about the feeling? The more mysterious or even confusing it was at the time, embrace it now and the shift you felt when you experienced it.

✦   What did it show you about what matters most to you?

Write about that memory in a journal if you'd like—or simply hold it in your heart and let it return to you as a place of calm.

Loving Guidance

Ask yourself~

✦*Have I ever felt quietly protected—even if I didn't understand it at the time?*

✦ *Have there been signs— people, or nudges that helped to guide me?*

Let one memory rise to the surface. If it brings emotion, allow that to move through you gently.

Really feel it.

Return to Center

✦ *Close your eyes and bring to mind a place that soothes you—a window, a garden, a certain room, or something symbolic like my greenhouse in my story.*

✦ *Let it become your sanctuary.*

✦ *Imagine yourself returning there any time you need peace. Feel it, anchor it.*

Say silently to yourself~

"I am safe to return to stillness. I am guided. I am loved."

Ask yourself~

Where have I experienced a sense of being guided — even when I didn't understand it at the time? or

What early experience can you remember that has shaped how I see myself, or what I believe is possible?

Let the answers come gently. Don't force, just listen.

Now bring to mind one moment from your life that held peace, beauty, or mystery, let yourself remember it fully.

Let that memory become a place you can return to anytime.

Let it ground you.

You may want to write about this moment in a journal—or simply hold it in your heart.

Let it remind you of who you really are beneath all the noise.

Chapter 2

When the Old You No Longer Fits

Finding Grace in the In-Between

Let your journey begin from a place of compassion and presence, where you can reconnect with the strength of your deeper self. When you live from this place, something opens.

You begin to feel your worth in a deeper way. You realize you're more deserving than you ever allowed yourself to believe. From that space of alignment, you start to welcome your true desires—not with guilt or hesitation, but with passion and purpose.

The Power That Was Always Yours

You are an infinite being— not limited by your past, your mistakes, or your pain. You are far more expansive than that. You're here to create and live the life your soul truly desires.

When you begin to see yourself as infinite, you realize healing isn't as much about effort—it's about remembering. That's where a consistent practice comes in. You don't need something complicated.

You need something simple—something that brings you back to clarity, love, and direction, especially when life feels chaotic.

Knowing There's a Way

Not knowing how to heal doesn't mean healing isn't meant for you.

You may not have found the right path yet–but it exists. You already carry a quiet connection to your higher self–it's always been there.

As you strengthen that connection, fear loosens its grip and true healing begins. At times, it may feel easier to stay in the familiar–even when it's uncomfortable. Many of us are more used to fear than alignment, so we tell ourselves it's okay to feel this way.

But you can begin to gently shift:

Choose calm.

Grow your confidence.

Allow abundance to flow naturally as you align with your true self.

The process you begin through this practice is unique to you–yet it's available to anyone who truly wants to grow and align more each day. It doesn't work better for one person than another.

The more you use it, the more naturally you'll grow in self-love, clarity, and purpose. From that space, you'll begin to attract what you've always known you truly deserve.

This is how you become a magnet for what you truly want–by expressing it without all the added fear and doubt. Fear and doubt are the primal emotions we're born with for survival, but they don't have to define your path.

Only you can truly know what your heart wants. And if you're not sure yet, that's okay. Clarity isn't something you're meant to have all at once. It comes gently over time, as you keep listening…

As you stay open, you start to notice the possibilities that have been there all along–quietly waiting for you.

No one else can create your path, but the moment you're ready to see it, it begins to unfold.

The noise of negative thoughts fades, a quiet settles in–and in that quiet, you feel free.

You begin to match the vibration of all the goodness life has to offer.

What is Your Truth?

"Until the unconscious becomes conscious, it will rule your life and you will call it fate."

~Carl Jung

Your truth is a part of you that's always creating–whether you realize it or not. Even when you're not fully aware, your energy is shaping what unfolds around you.

Each time you become more conscious, you step into greater alignment with your divine nature. From that place, fear begins to loosen its grip.

Healing begins.

Change becomes possible.

Throughout this book, I sometimes use the word

God, and other times I use terms like Source, Spirit, or divine energy. Please feel free to substitute the name that feels most aligned with your heart.

This work honors your unique relationship with the greater presence of love that guides and supports you.

Love is the opposite of fear.

It's stronger than fear.

As fear softens, your mind becomes clearer.

You become more open, and you receive more fully.

Each time you are aware and release an old, limiting belief, you make space for the life that's truly meant for you. From that space, your intuition begins to speak more clearly.

Your soul has been always listening.

It carries the vision–and the next steps–for who you're becoming.

Embodying Your Sacred Power

As you practice living as a conscious creator–
and as you embrace passion and purpose–you
begin to detach from scarcity, fear, and
reactivity. It's where you become more aligned
with your truth.

This is you remembering who you are. It's
where you begin to care for your soul self, and
to believe in what's possible. It's a process we
take day by day, growing in awareness and
staying open to receive.

It's where we give ourselves, our Higher Power,
other people, as well as the Universe permission
to send us the love we want and truly need.

You manifest a still mind. You're able to feel
more compassion, love more deeply, discover
your passions, and even make more money, (or
not)—all by creating a life that feels true to you
and doing what you love.

You create an environment you thrive in with
people and opportunities. You attract more

positive energy in all ways. The possibilities are limitless. You keep growing with what you create more of.

When Power Becomes Presence

We already practice discipline in many ways; we take care of our bodies, eat nourishing food, tend to our homes, and show up for others.

These habits keep us grounded and well.

Spiritual discipline is no different. It's about choosing what supports your highest wellbeing—even when it's not the easiest thing to do in the moment.

This isn't about control or perfection. It's about respect. You respect your time, your energy, and your spirit enough to care for them. You return to practices that bring you peace. You take the time to listen within.

Over time, this creates a deep, lasting shift. You begin to trust yourself more. You begin to feel different.

Remembering Who You Are

We are spiritual beings living in human bodies. But most of us lose touch with our spiritual identity early in life. We're shaped by ego, fear, and outside influences. We forget the clarity and power we were born with.

To return to your higher self takes intention. You don't have to force it, but you do need to want it. It helps to have something you know that works for you that makes it easier to stay connected.

It doesn't take years to feel a shift. Just a few weeks of steady practice can create a powerful difference. Many people find they can calm their mind and reconnect to peace within seconds after some consistency.

Tuning in becomes second nature. You stop getting pulled under by negativity. You stay steady in the face of chaos. You grow lighter, freer, and more intuitive. And you begin to recognize yourself again.

Understanding Your Dual Nature

"The intuitive mind is a sacred gift and the rational mind is a faithful servant. We have created a society

that honors the servant and has forgotten the gift."

~Albert Einstein

Inside you are two voices: one from the higher mind, and one from the ego. The ego is your lower consciousness. It reacts to fear and feeds off doubt. It generates thoughts that feel urgent, heavy, or dramatic—and often untrue. Its job is to keep you safe, but it does so by keeping you small.

Your higher consciousness is your soul self. It speaks with calm knowing. It doesn't need to shout. It helps you feel grounded, present, and connected to your purpose.

You are not meant to eliminate the ego—but to master it. To notice when it's speaking and choose not to allow it. To know when it's time to release it. That's where your power lives: in the space between the thought and how you respond to it.

Most of us go through life unaware of how powerful we are. When you don't know how to release fear, you end up waiting—for a solution, a sign, or someone else to lead the way.

But once you own your own power, you stop waiting. You start choosing. And things begin to change.

You are not a victim of your thoughts. You are not a prisoner of your past. You are not stuck.

When you choose to live consciously—detached from fear and aligned with your inner wisdom—you open the door to a different experience. One that feels lighter, clearer, and more true to who you are.

You stop chasing. You begin attracting.

You stop spinning. You begin receiving.

You stop surviving. You begin living.

Trusting the Path That's Unfolding for You

Your practice is your own personal healing process. You heal physically,

mentally/emotionally, and spiritually. You will learn how to create a sanctuary within your mind, as you use your practice to align with inner calm.

When chakras are unblocked and revitalized with energy work, strength flows through your spiritual and energetic systems. The renewed balance supports healing throughout your entire body– reaching your organs, cells, and even symptoms of illness.

This energy also heightens your awareness and intuition. As you receive, and the more open you become, the more you want to share what you have with others.

This is where you begin to create your life with intention. There's no failure, no mistakes—only growth with each step you take. You begin to feel free and aligned with your purpose. As you reconnect with who you are, joy comes more easily. You tap into your unlimited potential.

"The truth" is that you are more deserving than you realize! Every person on Earth is here to discover that truth for themselves. You access everything you dream of through higher consciousness and intuition. That's when you shift from reacting to life into consciously creating it.

When you align with your inner self, you naturally become more passionate. Your divine center is a safe, sacred place to create more of what is right for you.

Creating Your Sanctuary Within

Just because you haven't yet found a path to healing doesn't mean you weren't meant to heal. Sometimes, simply discovering that a way forward exists changes everything. After all, how could any of us know how to reconnect with the soul without a process that gently shows us the way?

14

You already have a direct line to your inner wisdom. As you strengthen that connection, fear begins to loosen its grip. We often stay in discomfort simply because it's familiar–the mind clings to what it knows—even if it's painful. But it's just as easy to start a new habit– one rooted in confidence and clarity.

When you use a practice that helps you feel calm and focused, you begin to rise. You step into new levels of awareness. You start to connect with your soul self, your truth.

Even the smallest ritual, done with openness, can connect you to higher clarity. You stop reacting from fear— and begin responding with confidence.

You don't need to force it. You don't need to be perfect and consistent with your new habits either. It doesn't matter where you begin.

Everyone starts somewhere.

What matters is the willingness to take one step at a time and to keep coming back to the present moment. The more you stay with it, the more you'll feel supported, steady, and free. The truth is, the things meant for you are already nearby.

You can recognize them—and receive them.

As the mind quiets, your real strength emerges.

You begin to remember:

You are already whole. You are enough.

Your soul is always creating, even when you're not fully aware. Each time you become more conscious, you connect to your inner divine, the presence of God within you. This is the source of energy that guides, creates, and restores.

If the word "God" doesn't resonate for you, that's okay. You can connect with the divine in your own way—through nature, a loving guide, or the higher intelligence of the universe. What matters is that it feels personal, safe, and loving to you.

Spirituality isn't about being better or having the "right" belief. It's about choosing to love as Source Energy loves—with presence, grace, and depth.

Your Soul Knows

Your soul doesn't think in terms of lack. It remembers what you are capable of. When you move beyond fear-based thoughts, you create more space in your mind and it opens to receive more creativity and possibility. With that space, you give yourself the freedom to grow beyond who you thought you were—expanding into new levels of soulful expression.

And you don't need to regret not starting sooner. What matters is that you're here now. Awareness is a form of healing. The moment you decide to be present, you shift your life's direction.

You've always been in a process, even when you were reacting unconsciously. But now, you're choosing to engage with that process on purpose. That's when everything begins to change.

Return to Yourself'

This isn't about becoming someone new. It's about becoming more fully yourself. As you start practicing conscious creation, you'll notice the difference between reacting from fear and responding with clarity. You'll detach more easily from worry, scarcity, and self-doubt—and return more quickly to your truth.

You begin to believe that good things are meant for you, and you stop resisting them. With each day of practice, you grow stronger in your ability to stay clearer and more centered.

You may find yourself setting new intentions, discovering hidden passions, or receiving help you didn't expect.

You'll also be able to shift more quickly into calm when things go wrong. That's the power of your inner sanctuary. It helps you navigate life with clarity instead of chaos.

When you align with this steady inner state, opportunities start to match your energy. People respond to your calm presence. You attract more of what lights you up—and less of what drains you.

The possibilities truly are limitless when you stay grounded in this space of clarity and trust.

Home to Yourself

Your unfolding carries you into brighter, more expansive places. It's your personal way of connecting, healing, and evolving. It's not a one-time event, but a continual becoming, You become more aligned with who you truly are.

Over time, your personal process begins to help your body and mind begin to attune to peace. Your nervous system strengthens. Your spirit feels safe again.

As you continue this work, you may notice pain lessening, anxiety lifting, or a deeper sense of connection.

These are real changes.

They don't happen because you force them—but because you allow yourself to receive them.

In time, your spiritual gifts will begin to reveal themselves—arriving naturally, when you're ready to receive them. They are gifts of protection, insight, and healing.

You begin living in flow, trusting that each step is guiding you forward. There are no wrong turns here.

Each step is useful.

Each moment of stillness is powerful.

There is no failure—only learning.

You are remembering how to live as your true self. You're learning to walk with presence and purpose. And as you continue this journey, your confidence will grow, not because you're perfect, but because you're finally connected.

What's the Purpose of This Life, Anyway?

I believe the purpose of this life is to remind ourselves– every day. To remember the truth of who we really are; divine beings with the power to heal, creating love.

We carry within us the ability to reconnect with the part of ourselves that already knows how to live in alignment–with peace, clarity, and joy.

It's knowing we are never alone.

You are supported.

You are guided.

You are meant to thrive.

When You're Caught in the In-Between

If you've ever found yourself in a season where nothing feels certain or familiar, you're not alone. Sometimes we do find ourselves in a season and it's not part of our plan. It can feel like a foggy space, impossible to navigate.

This too, can be part of the process. It's not about being lost—it's about learning to hold hope even when the future feels out of reach.

You may not yet believe that something better is possible. That feeling can be excruciating. You're not behind.

This tender in-between space is not the end—it's part of your unfolding. one that lives in the in-between. It's the space where you've let go of the version of yourself that once felt safe, but no longer works. It's where you haven't quite arrived fully at the life you're building, the one you're envisioning, planning for, and slowly creating.

You may not even have a map yet.

All you have is hope— the desire to have what you want.

It might be the hope to not feel so lost.

You feel raw and untethered.

You know you can't go back to numbing or performing–not now–but you also don't know how to move forward.

And the most painful part?

You don't yet believe you can create something better. You may not know where to begin. And the clarity and confidence you long for still feel out of reach.

That space is excruciating, because you're awake now, and there's no map.

But this too can be a part of the process. The ache, the confusion, the longing–they're signs that you're alive and reaching for something real.

You don't need to know what it looks like yet.

You just need to keep walking.

Where Healing Begins

We may not even realize how unaware we've become–moving through life in a state of observation rather than engagement. And when we are only observing, we can't fully recognize the opportunities in front of us. But when we are more aware, this opens the door to allowing.

And through allowing, we begin to accept.

When we're mainly observing, we're not doing, and if we're not doing—we're not creating. Without creation, we become stagnant. Energy is meant to move. But when we begin to use the gifts we've been given—no matter how small—life begins to move with more ease.

We can open a direct line to the energy of the universe—a living current of healing and support. Receiving and working with this energy isn't just a spiritual idea; it's an act of trust. It's how we remember we're never alone, and that something sacred is always available to guide us.

This isn't passive.

You're not waiting to be rescued. You're cocreating your life— on purpose, with presence.

When you stay open to what's available to you, things begin to shift. You feel held. Even through life's rougher moments, everything moves with more grace.

Living, Falling, Rising, Becoming

Life isn't linear. We stumble, we soar, we start over. But no matter where we are, there is always a way forward.

"Begin anywhere."

~John Cage

You are meeting yourself exactly where you need to be–not broken, not behind. You're whole, and you're learning to stand in your truth, instead of your fear. You don't need to have it all figured out. You just need to begin.

There's more strength in you than you know—in showing up, in practicing, and in learning how to rest.

You don't need to be perfect.

You don't need to have it all figured out.

You just need to begin.

This strength builds with practice. Each time you return to presence, you move closer to your true self.

✦ Practice With Me: Begin From Where You Are

This practice is a gentle invitation to begin walking your path as a conscious creator—not through striving, but through connection.

Close your eyes for a moment. Let your breath be soft and steady.

Notice where you are—not just physically, but emotionally and energetically.

Are you tired?

Feeling stuck?

Hopeful?

Unsure?

There's no wrong answer.

✦ *Now whisper gently to yourself~*

✦ *"I am allowed to begin from here."*

✦ *You don't need a perfect mindset or a flawless plan.*

You just need a breath—and trust.

✦ *Feel your feet on the ground. Imagine energy flowing from beneath the earth through your feet, and all 7 chakras, all the way to the top of your head.*

✦ *Breath softly. With each inhale, invite in strength.*

✦ *With each exhale, release pressure and expectation.*

✦ *You're not behind.*

✦ *You are in process— and that's sacred.*

✦ *Sit with this truth for a few moments.*

✦ *Let it settle.*

✦ *When you're ready, open your eyes.*

✦ *You've already begun.*

✦ **Repeat softly** *out loud or within your heart~*

✦ *"My soul is already aligned with truth."*

✦

   "I am safe to remember who I am."

✦ *"I create with love."*

✦ *"I choose with intention."*

✦ *"I receive peace."*

Feel the energy coming through you. Let yourself feel the possibility of something shifting, even if you can't name it yet.

Soul Inquiry

Take a few moments to reflect—or write in a journal what comes to you—on the questions below—

✦   *Where have I been reacting from fear or old patterns?*

✦   *Where am I ready to respond with clarity and presence?*

✦
Ask yourself—

What would it look like to connect with my healing, not to fix myself, but to reconnect with my truth, my soul?

There are no wrong answers. Be honest and allow yourself to be present. This is about presence, not perfection.

Begin Your Practice

✦ *Choose one small practice to begin today— something that says, "I want to connect." It might be:*

✦ *Sitting in stillness for two minutes and simply breathing slowly, exhaling fully.*

✦ *Placing your hand over your heart and noticing how you feel.*

✦ *Saying "I choose calm" next time tension arises.*

✦

It's where you're letting go of something that's been weighing on your energy.

This is how you start your practice—not with control, but with love.

You aren't becoming someone else. You are remembering who you are and being that way.

◆

Chapter 3

The Power of Desire and How to Work with It

Your desires are your soul's invitation to grow and align with the life waiting for you. In this chapter you'll learn how to welcome them with compassion, listen to their guidance, and stay connected to love instead of fear.

Desire is a spiritual force. It's not a flaw—it's how we evolve.

At first, longing can feel raw. It often begins with simply wanting something—more freedom, more ease, more connection.

At its highest level, desire is about aligning with your divine nature—your soul self that already contains everything you need. When you begin creating from a deeper place—from what feels right, not just what you've been taught—desire becomes a practice.

✦ *But as you heal and awaken, your desire naturally expands into something greater:*

✦ *A wish to serve.*

✦ *To give.*

✦ *To create from love.*

When you say yes to life, life responds.

It asks how it can serve you, too.

You Deserve What You Want

When a longing arises, it's a sign you're ready to explore it. You'll recognize what's right by how it feels:

Clear.

Grounded.

Alive.

Desire was here long before you were born and continues into infinity. But not all desire is conscious.

Ask yourself: is this what I truly want—or what I've been taught to chase?

If your desires feel obsessive or anxious, pause and detach.

Stay open.

Try not to cling to what you're used to, since something better shows up when you least expect it—something deeper—something even better than what you imagined.

Desire for Alignment Takes Practice

When you tune into your quiet mind and visualize with peace, you create a vibrational match with what's right for you.

This work builds over time. Each time you shift a thought, detach from an obsessive loop, or tune in to receive energy, you strengthen your alignment.

It takes seconds to shift, but consistency strengthens your connection. Over time, your thoughts, energy, and emotions start aligning more naturally.

You'll feel calmer.

More clear.

More grounded.

You don't have to practice perfectly.

You can forget for a month and still come back and make real progress. As long as you keep returning, you'll keep expanding.

The first time you experience your still mind and see how powerful it is, you'll want to keep going. The key is to let yourself evolve without pressure.

Keep practicing.

Even a quick moment of connection can open you to a day of peace.

You Attract What You Focus On

It's not what you want that creates change—it's what you focus on and truly believe. The universe responds to that. When your thoughts are centered around lack, that energy is mirrored back to you.

Shift your attention to what you **do** want. Let your thoughts become a magnet for the future you're creating.

Write down what you truly want. What you desire comes from your heart, not your fear. Let your imagination show you what's possible when you believe in yourself!

Let Yourself Grow Beyond What Feels Familiar

Growth often begins with discomfort. The desire to grow is real, but it's easy to resist leaving the safety of what's familiar, even if that comfort zone is no longer serving us. Sometimes, what we're craving isn't a specific outcome—it's the *feeling* we believe that outcome will give us.

Stay open. Sometimes what comes is even better than what you first imagined. As you practice this openness, you'll get better at discerning what's truly aligned and what's not.

Move Past Doubt and into Your Power

Fear and doubt show up whenever we're on the edge of transformation. That doesn't mean you're on the wrong path. It means you're expanding.

You don't need to eliminate fear—you just need to stop giving it power.

✦ *Ask yourself~*

✦ *What have I been doing just to survive–not to thrive?*

✦ *Where have I allowed fear to shape my relationships, career, or decisions?*

✦ *What do I want to release?*

✦ *What do I wish to welcome?*

The universe is ready to respond to your clarity.

Choose creation over stagnation.

Each time we ignore our desires or let fear dominate, we become stuck. We blame our circumstances. We replay past failures. We get caught in the belief that life is happening to us rather than through us.

But stagnation is a symptom—not your truth.

You have the power to shift. You are not defined by what has happened.

Your imagination is a portal to a new reality. Assume the version of you that's already living with clarity, confidence, and trust.

That's the energy that transforms everything!

Desire Isn't Selfish—It's Sacred

"Be Joyful Always; pray continually; give thanks in

all circumstances."

~Thessalonians 5:16-18

I use a mug for my tea that has this proverb written on it to remind me to be grateful. Gratitude isn't always spontaneous as we think it should be. Many times it needs to be cultivated through daily habits to remind you to look for the good.

Desire is not about materialism or ego—it's a call to connect with your soul, to feel gratitude and become more fully who you are. You may seek material abundance—and even after it's achieved, you may discover that true satisfaction emerges from simplicity and clarity.

Research has shown that those who choose voluntary simplicity often report higher wellbeing because simplicity cultivates purpose, connection, and alignment with one's values.

Others find joy in richness, complexity, or creative abundance, and both paths are valid. What matters is honoring your nature and living your truth, not performing for others, but instead being present with your soul and aligning with it.

Warren Buffett famously observed that money doesn't change people—it magnifies who they already are. When someone is generous, wealth amplifies that generosity; if self-centered, it underscores that trait.

Just as money magnifies who you already are, so desire—when filtered through spirituality—can reveal the depth of your soul. It can elevate intimacy beyond the purely physical.

That soul work invites a union where spirit and sensuality naturally intertwine. It's where sex practiced with love becomes sacred.

When sex is absent spiritually, it risks devolving into something primal and ego-driven—serving desire rather than expressing love.

Conscious Desire Creates

You're not here to live a small life. You're here to create from love, to trust your intuition, and to expand into your fullness.

Try saying~

"I'm here for my highest good."

"I stay open to light, ease, and grace."

Let that guide you when things feel challenging. You are always growing, even when you don't feel it.

Each moment is a chance to choose differently: to forgive, to let go, and to move toward the life that's calling you.

You Are Creating the Life You Desire

"The people who get on in this world are the people who get up and look for the circumstances they want, and if they can't find them, make them."

~Bernard Shaw

You are creating the life you desire. Keep choosing what aligns with your highest truth.

✦ **Practice With Me: Choosing Joy, Choosing Focus**

✦ *Take a quiet moment to pause.*

✦ *Let your breath slow.*

✦ *Let your mind soften.*

✦ *Now gently ask yourself~*

✦ *Where has my focus been lately?*

✦ *Have I been feeling fear—or feeling joy?*

No need to judge—just notice.

No pressure…no fixing. Just awareness.

Now say to yourself, softly~

"I am allowed to want more ease."

"I am allowed to feel joy."

"I choose to focus on what lifts me—even in small ways."

✦ *Take a slow breath in.*

✦ *As you exhale, imagine releasing any pressure to have it all figured out.*

✦ *Let your next thought be light.*

✦ *Let it be soft.*

✦ *Let it open a new possibility.*

✦*Then, whenever you're ready,* **say~**

"I am here for my highest good."

"I stay open to light, ease, and grace–even when things feel uncertain."

This is the beginning of joyful creation.

Not by force...

But by focus.

Chapter 4

How to Begin: A Ritual for Clearing, Centering, and Receiving

Knowing your desire gives you direction—but it's presence and practice that help you receive.

Now that you've begun to clarify what you truly want, it's time to clear some space for it. You don't have to know everything right away. You simply need a way to return to stillness and reconnect with your calm.

Your practice isn't about performance. It isn't about perfection either. It's about grounding your intention with compassion and giving your nervous system and spirit a safe place to land.

It's a sacred space you create, one that gently clears the noise and strengthens the connection to the wisdom within.

In the pages ahead, I'll share how to use a practice that you create that blends visualization, energy work, and everyday practical tools to support you in releasing what's weighing you down, so you can reconnect with the calm that's already yours.

The initial tool—what I call the *Primal Tool or Slide Projector Method*—helps release subconscious emotional patterns. These feelings are often rooted in early conditioning, stored deeply in your energy field.

Once they're released, you're no longer carrying the weight of someone else's pain or influence.

The rest of your practice flows more easily.

You then can use everyday tools that take just seconds to help to release negative thoughts and emotional overwhelm throughout the day. Your gentle practices shift you from fear to clarity and confidence. They are especially helpful when you're just beginning, as you may be more sensitive during this stage of healing.

As your practice deepens, you'll start to feel more protected and safer in your own energy. You'll begin to receive guidance through your intuition and feel more confident in your everyday decisions.

You'll sense energy flowing through you—from the top of your head where your crown is, your portal, reminding you that you are always supported.

When you sit down to receive energy that comes from beneath the Earth through your feet, it helps to unblock tired and stuck chakras and restore you. It relieves fatigue, increases clarity, and even brings physical healing.

It helps you feel like yourself again.

You don't have to do this perfectly. Even once a week, or even once a month, can create a powerful shift. The more consistently you practice, the faster you progress. But even infrequent use can bring life-changing results.

Begin to love yourself more.

See others through a lens of compassion.

Attract what's truly aligned.

Heal—body, mind, and soul.

How This Practice Helps You Shift

"Insanity is doing the same thing over and over and

expecting a different result."

~Albert Einstein

You are not a product of your past. You are who you choose to be now. You, aligned with your deeper truth and intuition. As you begin to trust yourself, you break the cycle of old patterns— and gently step out of your familiar suffering— and into possibility.

This is where your miracle begins.

Why the Tools Are Sacred?

The tools are sacred because they're activated by your intention. Each use is a yes—to clarity, peace, and emotional freedom.

With practice, you'll know how to stay detached from fear, self-doubt, guilt, anger, low self-worth, and any other excess emotional state that has been clouding your peace.

You'll begin to notice more stillness in your mind.

In that stillness, it becomes easier to respond with clarity, rather than react from old wounds.

You begin to know yourself more deeply.

You begin to move through life with greater grace.

Awareness Is Your Superpower

Wisdom is knowing which thoughts to keep— and choosing to release the rest.

When a negative emotion arises, pause and ask:

What thought is behind this feeling?

Awareness allows you to step back and reclaim your peace.

You don't have to force anything.

Just notice.

Once you become aware, you can make a deliberate shift by choosing not to attach. You can release the thought, emotion, or pattern that doesn't serve you.

It doesn't matter how busy your life is. It doesn't matter who you are. Everyone has the power to create clarity.

How to Use Awareness Throughout the Day

At the beginning, it helps to sit down to meditate and receive energy at least once to a few times per week—even if just for a few minutes. You can always go deeper when time allows.

When life feels too busy to sit down for a full meditation, you can still stay open with awareness. You can stay open as you walk, drive, or work. Any time you stay open to God or what is divine to you, you are in prayer.

You can visualize light. You can mentally release what's blocking you and quickly call in fresh energy.

These simple, subtle moments are powerful.

They create real change.

Over time, you'll become more aware of how one small thought can shift your energy. When a thought feels heavy or draining, you can choose to release it—or gently replace it with one that feels lighter. This simple shift can lift your vibration instantly. The more you practice, the more natural it becomes.

Return to Calm

You don't need to fix the problem—you just need to return to calm.

Sometimes anxiety comes from something specific–a recent conversation, a stressful memory, or a real challenge you're facing.

Other times, it stems from a familiar thought pattern that pulls you down without you even realizing it. Whether the trigger seems big or small, the effect can be heavy. That's why this practice matters.

Even the smallest reaction is worth noticing.

If it disrupts your peace, it's worth releasing.

You'll stop spinning in the same mental loops that used to drain you, and start living from your deeper calm.

✦ **Practice With Me: Clearing, Centering & Receiving**

This ritual is a doorway—

A sacred invitation to return to yourself and reconnect with your inner calm.

Create Sacred Space

Before you begin, take a moment to set your space with intention. You don't need candles or tools—just presence.

✦ *Sit or lie in a quiet place.*

✦ *Close your eyes and place one hand over your heart.*

✦ *Let your breath slow.*

✦ *Allow yourself to be supported by the light around you.*

✦ *Say aloud~*

"I am open to healing."

"I am safe to release."

"I am safe to receive."

After speaking these words, gently affirm your willingness to receive, to release, and to heal.

Let this intention settle into your body.

Then ask yourself~

How do I feel now compared to before I began?

Chapter 5

Create with Intention and Sensitivity

When you create with intention, you become a magnet for higher frequencies. Your reality begins to shift to align with your inner peace. Even in times of stress or uncertainty, you can learn to create a sacred space beyond the reach of the ego.

You can shift to this sacred place anytime. The more you live from that truth, the more you tap into your own bliss.

Longing, Hoping, Believing → Claiming and

Receiving

We all come into this life with desire—longing for something, needing something, crying out for connection.

Over time, we learn to trust that our needs will be met.

When we can, we give. When we're able, we receive.

This rhythm of longing and giving is part of being human—and part of being in spirit. It's how we grow.

Believe that something beautiful is meant for you.

This belief is not just wishful thinking–it's an act of alignment. It's where you align your thoughts and actions and meet with kindness, clarity, and love. It's how you create a space for what you want to appear.

Sometimes we drift off course. We forget our power. We move through life only half-aware of what we truly want—or who we really are. We tell ourselves we're fine. That we don't need anything. Or we let guilt, fear, or shame keep us from claiming our deeper longings.

This quiet denial limits us. On the other end of the spectrum, we might get caught up in material striving—always reaching, always wanting, never feeling satisfied. This too pulls us away from presence and gratitude. But you can return at any time.

Instead of pushing or denying, pause. Focus on what you truly want—and what you're grateful for.

Stay open, and you'll begin to see opportunities where you once only saw obstacles. You cannot feel deeply connected to your truth while living in a state of fear or lack.

But when you remember who you are—and begin living as the version of you, who already feels peaceful and grateful—you step into your creative power.

You start to believe in yourself, even before the outer evidence appears. That's what faith looks like.

As it says in James 2:26~

"For as the body without the spirit is dead, so faith

without work is dead also."

When you stay open to Source, and allow your practice to support you, you create a powerful anchor for your life.

Creating peace in your life is not about perfection—it about presence.

It's an act of loving responsibility to yourself.

You are allowed to choose what feels true.

You are allowed to receive what you long for.

✦ Practice With Me: Knowing Desire

Desire is not a flaw—it's the soul's invitation to grow and create through love.

This practice is here to help you recognize what you're truly longing for, and begin to welcome it. without pressure.

Honor What You Want~

✦ *Close your eyes, take 3 slow breaths. Let your body soften.*

✦ **Ask yourself~**

What am I truly longing for right now, not what I think I should want, but what my soul really craves?

This could be anything such as peace, freedom, purpose, clarity, improved health, or something tangible like a beautiful home that feels safe.

✦ **Now gently ask~**

How have I been trying to survive instead of create?

✦ *Notice what comes to you.*

✦ *Observe. Don't feel you have to fix anything.*

Welcome Clarity

Desire in alignment is about focus, not pressure.

Where you place your attention is what begins to grow.

✦ *Take a moment to write or reflect on these things~*

✦ *What am I ready to release that no longer supports who I'm becoming?*

✦ *Am I ready to welcome what fulfills me, even if it feels uncomfortable or unfamiliar because it's different from what I'm used to?*

✦ Remember, you are allowing, not pushing.

Choose to Stay Open Instead of Fear

Say~

"I am open to the life I am meant to live."

"I am open to being guided."

"I am open to receiving what aligns with my highest good."

Let yourself sit in this openness for a few minutes. You may feel emotion—that's okay.

Desire asks us to expand, and this can be uncomfortable at first.

This is not about doing this perfectly, it's more about being willing —that intentional moment you create right now.

How do I access and trust my intuition?

Everyone has intuitive abilities. You don't need to wait for a mystical moment or a sign. Your inner guidance is already within you.

If you've ignored your intuition in the past, or doubted yourself, it's not too late to strengthen this connection. Maybe your intuitive nudges come as gut feelings, or flashes of insight.

Maybe you're an empath who feels everything. Or you've had dreams or visions that defy explanation.

✦   *Instead of questioning it, pause and notice. Stop over analyzing.*

✦   **Ask yourself,**

✦   *What was my first feeling?*

✦   *What did I already know before I second-guessed it?*

The more you trust your instincts, the clearer they become.

Some people experience intuitive hits through sound, smell, images, or energetic sensations.

Others receive clear insight during meditation.

Sensitivity is not a weakness—it's a gift.

As you learn to stay grounded, cleanse energy that's not yours, and set boundaries, your intuition becomes a powerful ally.

The more you tune in, the more natural this inner guidance becomes. In time, you'll no longer wonder if it's real. You'll simply know.

✦ Practice With Me: Create With Sensitivity and Intuition

You are a conscious creator. What you feel, focus on, and embody shapes the reality that unfolds around you.

This practice helps you reconnect with your creative power by honoring your sensitivity as a divine tool—not a flaw.

Come Home to Alignment

✦ *Let yourself soften starting with your shoulders.*

✦ Place your hands wherever you feel most
   sensitive—your heart, your solar plexus, your
   temples—and **repeat silently:**

"My sensitivity is not too much."

"It is the channel through which truth arrives." ✦
Notice what begins to shift inside as you speak.

✦ Do this gently, no rush.

✦ Tune into Your Intuition

✦ Close your eyes and ask gently~

✦ How does my intuition speak to me most clearly?

✦ Is it through sound or music?

✦ Is it through sudden images or color flashes?

✦Through sensations—goosebumps, chills, warmth?

✦ *Is there an emotional knowing or a subtle inner nudge that is so strong you want to pay more attention?*

Observe~

No need to decide anything.

You may begin to notice a dominant channel more in the next few days.

Now ask yourself~

What has fear or lack (thoughts and feelings) been distracting me from receiving?

Shift to a Creative Frequency

Think of a simple soul-aligned desire or intention that's in your heart.

Feel what it feels like to long for it.

✦ *Shift your focus away on the "how" or "when" and instead shift to~*

✦ *How would it feel to already have this reality?*

✦ *What can I do today however small it is that*
  brings me into alignment with that feeling?

Even a 1% shift matters.

Manifestation doesn't come through control. It
comes through truth.

Chapter 6

Your Process is Sacred

Embrace your unfolding path, trust your timing, and deepen your connection with your inner sanctuary.

Transformation can feel like floating down a river on an inner tube—sometimes smooth, sometimes slow and stillness. Just like life, there are ebbs and flows. When you find yourself in an ebb, don't stop doing the work. It may feel stagnant or unchanging, but even stillness is alive with potential. With openness, shifts will come—sometimes quickly, sometimes when least expected.

What often blocks the flow is the unconscious reel of fear and scarcity. These beliefs can freeze everything in its place. But even a small shift in awareness can bring you back into alignment. It only takes a few seconds, or a single breath, to change the energy of your day.

We don't experience life as it is—we experience what we focus on. That's why I like to call it *doing the work*—not for perfection, but for your own bliss.

The work itself is simple. It's remembering, in the present moment, to shift a thought that would otherwise keep you stuck. At first, this might feel unfamiliar. But with intention and practice, it becomes second nature. A few moments of awareness can redirect your entire day.

Where focus goes, energy flows. If you dwell on what's lacking or irritating, your experience will reflect that. But within you is deeper consciousness—your inner observer—who knows how to stay grounded, centered, and detached. That knowing is already inside you, waiting to be activated.

Your process is about awareness. You will have tough days, everyone does. Don't let your ego convince you that you're failing. Every effort

counts. You are creating something sacred—
your own evolving path.

Happiness comes from the willingness to move
into the unknown. It means choosing love over
fear, calm over chaos. It's trusting that you are
exactly where you're meant to be.

As you rise in vibration, you naturally attract
more peace, beauty and clarity. You begin to see
imagination as a tool for creation. You start to
believe that life is unfolding for your highest
good.

In the beginning, it might feel easier to retreat
into old patterns, especially fear. The ego may
tell you that staying small is safer, or that others'
needs come first. But that path becomes heavier
over time.

Living in fear is exhausting. Awareness brings
lightness. You can't solve a problem with the
same mind that created it. Choosing to stay
open is an act of courage, and of grace.

As your practice deepens, you might feel like a different person. You're still you—but now with a peaceful mind, empowered thoughts, and a calm presence.

Old triggers lose their grip. The thoughts, people, and situations that once weighed you down will no longer define you.

Habits shift. Happiness starts to feel natural.

Alignment is not a destination; it's a choice. It's choosing what feels connected and true in this moment.

Letting your mind settle.

Letting your energy rise.

Letting go of what no longer fits.

When you do, life begins to meet you with more grace. This is where you receive the gifts meant for you. This is where your purpose becomes clear—and you finally get to live it.

✦ Practice With Me: The Power of Choice

In this moment—and every moment—you have the power to choose.

✦ *Take a slow breath in and exhale.*

✦ *Place one hand on your heart.*

✦ *Say, "In this moment, I choose calm. I choose presence. I choose to remember who I am."*

✦ Practice With Me: Begin Anywhere

This next practice invites you to go deeper.

Start by noticing the quality of the voice inside you.

Is it calm and loving—or urgent, doubtful, afraid?

This is how you begin to sense whether your higher self or your ego is guiding you.

Anchor into Presence ✦

Sit comfortably.

✦ *Feel your feet on the floor*

✦ *Feel your breath moving in and out*

✦ *Ask gently:*

Which voice am I listening to right now?

✦ Ego often speaks through fear, doubt, urgency, or exaggerated emotion.

✦ It tends to dramatize, or distort your center.

✦ Your higher self feels calm, grounded, steady.

✦ It holds a quiet knowing that things will work out.

You're not here to judge your thoughts–you're here to observe. You're learning to become the observer so you can gently release what no longer serves you.

Throughout the day, be aware of sudden shifts in emotion—worry, sadness, fear, or anger.

When they arise, ask~

Do I need to be thinking about this right now?

Is there something I need to do–or am I just reacting?

If not--pause.

✦ *Close your eyes.*

✦ *Look at the thought or feeling.*

✦ **Say~**

✦ *"I don't have to hold you right now."*

✦ **Practice With Me: Create with Sensitivity and Intuition**

You are a conscious creator.

What you feel, focus on, and embody shapes what unfolds around you.

This practice helps you reconnect with your creative power by honoring your sensitivity as a divine tool—not a flaw.

Come home to alignment.

Let yourself soften starting with your shoulders.

Place your hands wherever you feel most sensitive; your heart, your solar plexus, your temples—and *repeat silently~*

"My sensitivity is not too much."

"It is the channel through which truth arrives."

Notice what begins to shift inside as you speak.

Do this gently, no rush.

Tune into your intuition.

*Close your eyes and **ask gently~***

How does my intuition speak to me most clearly?

Is it through sound or music?

Is it through sudden images or color flashes?

Through sensations —goosebumps, chills, warmth?

An emotional knowing or a subtle inner nudge that is so strong you want to pay more attention?

Observe.

No need to decide anything.

You may begin to notice a dominant channel more in the next few days.

Now ask yourself~

✦ *What has fear or lack (thoughts and feelings) been distracting me from receiving?*

Shift to a creative frequency.

✦ *Think of a simple soul-aligned desire or intention that's in your heart.*

✦ *Feel what it feels like to long for it.*

✦ *Shift your focus away on the "how" or "when" and instead shift to knowing.*

✦ *How would it feel to already have this reality?*

✦ *What can I do today however small it is that brings me into alignment with that feeling?*

Even a 1% shift matters.

Using a tool to release fear or doubt that doesn't serve you.

✦ *Close your eyes.*

Say,

"Ego, I release your feeling of (doubt or fear, or any negative emotion that is strong) and this thought, (name the thought that came with it)—and

RELEASE."

✦ *Give it time to respond to your command.*

✦ *Watch as the excess negative energy begins to fade and move away from you. It might vibrate or become more distant.*

✦ Next, shift your focus: to your solar plexus, and
then your heart.

✦ Feel the shift into calm — the neutral space within
you.

✦ Bring to mind something divine–a symbol, nature,
or an image that represents love.

✦ Bring your awareness to your solar plexus and
then your heart.

✦ Become aware of how your thinking changes over
time, and how neutral you mind becomes,
connected to calm, even forgetting how you used to
think and even obsess with fear, doubt, hate, and
anger.

✦ Enjoy your new sanctuary within your mind. You
are the one creating this.

Say~

"I am grateful for this shift."

90

"I am free."

Remember this tool when doubt arises~

Each time you choose calm over chaos, you

reclaim your power.

Chapter 7

Energy Awareness

Learn how to sense and shift energy so you can stay calm, clear, and connected—no matter where you are or what's happening around you.

When you practice gratitude and begin creating from that space, you naturally return to your center. Over time, you stop judging yourself so harshly. You begin to see that everything serves a purpose—even the harder moments.

Judgment only keeps old patterns alive. Each time you catch yourself criticizing something, whether it's yourself, someone else, or a situation—gently shift your focus to gratitude. Let light stream through the thought. It was never truly yours to begin with.

You already hold everything you've ever needed.

As you continue this path of self-awareness, remember that healing doesn't mean forgetting the past–it means shifting your relationship to it. We often base our reality on a current challenge or a memory from long ago. It's a skill to let the past stay in the past. Mastering the art of letting go is how you reclaim your power.

We don't forget, but we can choose to release the weight of what no longer serves us. Holding onto resentment or fear only magnifies it. Your mind may even exaggerate a past event, making it worse than it was.

Many of your daily reactions aren't based on the present moment. They come from habit—a pattern of thinking and responding that's been repeated over time. This is the energetic pattern you've been conditioned to respond to—but in truth, the thoughts and emotions you focus on now shape the life you're living.

When we lose touch with gratitude, we often remain in a "safe zone," familiar, but heavy. It feels easier to notice what's wrong, and before we know it, we're living in survival mode.

We may tell ourselves that clinging to old ways of reacting, will protect us from pain—but that's ego, whispering its worn-out story.

Gratitude, on the other hand, breaks through even the darkest belief. It quiets the part of us that edges God out—the part that wants to keep us small or afraid.

Start with gratitude for the smallest thing. In any mundane moment, say, "I'm grateful for..." and fill in the blank.

Let yourself truly feel it. Over time, this simple act becomes transformational.

When you feel blocked, and as you use gratitude— also use a release tool if needed—to let light in.

Let it dissolve the burden, fear, anger, or need to be right. That moment of awareness and shift can be instantaneous.

You can also access gratitude through nature.

Notice what you'd usually miss— the rustling leaves, a passing bird, the scent of jasmine. Stop worrying about what you're going to say. Instead, listen more deeply to others. Smile, even when you don't feel like it.

These quiet acts open you to stillness and allow you to receive—to accept the gifts that come your way. This new world that you create becomes a reflection of what you believe.

Spiritual "Spaces"

We each move through different "spiritual spaces" depending on our current mindset and intentions. These spaces are influenced by our external circumstances, inner beliefs, and the choices we make. Understanding them can help us extend compassion, to ourselves and others.

Negative Space / Positive Thrust

Someone in a negative space with a positive thrust may be struggling, but they're trying to shift. Their energy might still feel heavy, but underneath it is an honest desire to move forward.

Negative Space / Negative Thrust

A person stuck in negativity with no intention to grow may resist change. Some may appear falsely positive, but their core energy reveals otherwise. While anyone can change, the longer they stay in this space, the harder it becomes to shift.

Positive Space / Negative Thrust

Some people appear upbeat, but are pulled by internal resistance. They may not want to fully hold onto their positivity. This creates conflict, but it can be redirected with awareness and gratitude.

Positive Space / Positive Thrust

This is alignment—where someone feels positive and is consciously choosing to stay that way. These individuals tend to be more grounded, conscious, and uplifting. They inspire others without effort.

We don't always consciously choose our space. Life's events—loss, illness, sudden changes—can pull us in different directions. Even receiving too much too soon can create imbalance. But we always have the power to return to ourselves.

Not everyone shows their space clearly. Some who seem negative may just be hurting. Some who appear cheerful may be masking something deeper. That's why empathy matters. We never truly know what someone else is carrying.

The more we understand these internal

"spaces," the more gently we can treat ourselves—and the more compassion we bring to this world.

✦ Practice With Me: Stay With Yourself

You don't have to know everything.

You don't have to keep up with anything or move quickly.

You only have to stay with yourself.

✦. *Find a comfortable quiet place to sit. Place your feet on the ground.*

✦ *Allow a pillar of strong white light to come from beneath the Earth and flow through the soles of your feet. Let it move upward through your body— gently clearing each of your chakras, one by one.*

✦ *Start at the first chakra and follow the light as it rises through the second, third, fourth, fifth, sixth, and finally the seventh chakra at the crown.*

✦ *As the light reaches the top of your head, allow it to exit through the seventh chakra and flow out the back of your head—through the energy portal at the base of your skull.*

✦ *Feel the light connecting you to something greater with protection.*

✦ *Feel yourself centered, grounded, and clear.*

Say~

✦*"I am safe to stay with myself."*

✦ **Then say~**

✦*"I am enough."*

Chapter 8

Protect Your Inner Sanctuary

The moment you begin to practice awareness, a quiet sanctuary begins to form within you. The more you protect that space, the more it grows. This is where you use your mind — *instead of letting your mind use you*!

If someone tries to draw you into an argument or into a toxic conversation, remember:

✦ You don't have to engage. You can choose to stay centered, stay silent, or walk away.

✦ Silence isn't weakness; it's protection.

✦ You're not avoiding the issue—you're preserving your peace.

✦ You're protecting your **inner sanctuary**.

Be vigilant. Don't allow the outer world to dictate what you think or how you feel. Don't get swept up by the media, the crowd, the fear— or the fear of what others might think of you.

Be Your Own Leader

When you know who you are and respect yourself, that's what matters most.

Studies have shown that when people are uncertain about what to do in a morally questionable situation, most do nothing. The same thing holds true in a crowd; if no one helps when someone is being hurt, the rest of the group often stand by.

This reveals something about human nature: we tend to follow the lead of others unless we're deeply rooted in our values. That's why it's essential to know yourself and act with integrity. When we teach this to our children, we help raise the collective consciousness.

During WWII, only a small number of soldiers refused to participate in genocide when given the choice. Many didn't want to comply, but they were so overwhelmed by the pressure that they chose not to decide. Later, many of them were left with lifelong regret.

Doing nothing is a decision—and many of us make that same decision every day in smaller ways, without even realizing it. We often don't even know what we're capable of until we're tested.

Very few people can handle being socially rejected or criticized.

But the more connected you are to your higher self, the more you trust yourself— and draw strength from within.

Become a Master of Your Thoughts

"Be careful about what you think, because your

thoughts run your life."

~Proverbs 4:23

Say to yourself~

"I am the master of my thoughts."

And believe it—because it's true.

Most of us have spent our lives reacting to our thoughts and emotions without knowing there's another way. But your thoughts create your experience, and you can choose which ones to focus on.

Even when we make mistakes or regress, we're still learning. Life's challenges help us grow and make better decisions. You won't always get it right, and that's okay.

Forgive yourself. Be gentle. Life isn't always meant to be easy—it's meant to be mastered.

"Your Imagination Is God."

~ Neville Goddard

Create Your Vision

Believe that you already are everything you hope to become. Think of someone you admire, someone whose qualities you respect.

Begin to see those same qualities in yourself.

If you've ever felt a twinge of envy, it may be because you recognize a truth: you already have those same qualities inside you, waiting to be claimed.

As your imagination expands, so does your sense of potential. When you become a "seer," you begin to notice how habitual thoughts no longer serve you. Desperate times often open the door to new insight. These uncomfortable moments can lead to powerful breakthroughs.

Become a Seer

With practice, you begin to glimpse your highest potential. You gain perspective and begin to forget the small reactive thoughts that used to occupy your mind.

At first, you notice that you're no longer thinking the same way. Later, those old patterns simply fall away. You'll still have emotional responses, but you no longer hold on to what doesn't need attention.

Your mind becomes more peaceful.

Turmoil fades, replaced by a greater understanding.

You rise to a new plateau—and then another...

What once felt like fear now becomes a doorway to possibility.

You begin to focus less on what could go wrong and more on what can go right. You're connected with a calm and understanding that feels more real than anything else.

How Do We Heal the Subconscious?

Before we can release old patterns in the unconscious, we have to understand where they come from—and how this subconscious mind actually works.

How Does the Subconscious Work?

As a child, you absorbed the emotions and beliefs of those around you. You didn't yet have the ability to challenge them, so you internalized them—especially the negative ones.

These emotions may lie dormant in your subconscious, waiting quietly until something, or someone, reactivates them.

That's why you might overreact or feel overwhelmed at times, it's not just the present moment triggering you—it's your unhealed past.

Stored emotions like fear, self-doubt, anger, shame, and the belief that you're not good enough form a false identity. This is not your truth. It's called the "illusion of self."

They shape how you see yourself–not through truth, but through ego and survival.

By releasing these patterns at the subconscious level, you gain clarity. You begin to respond rather than react and rationalize.

Your higher self becomes stronger than your old programming.

You move through life with greater ease.

How to Release Negativity from the Unconscious

The subconscious mind controls more than 97% of your reality. Releasing energy at this level helps dissolve blocks held in your root chakra and energy field—blocks that interfere with your connection to your inner calm.

We can learn to free ourselves from the mental "reel" of limiting beliefs. The fastest way to shift your reality is to shift your inner beliefs.

What we believe we deserve is what we allow ourselves to receive.

As you clear fear-based beliefs from your subconscious, you begin to change.

What once triggered you now passes by unnoticed.

You feel lighter, stronger, and more confident.

What's the First Step to Releasing from the Subconscious?

There are usually four to eight people from your early life who had a deep emotional impact—often in painful or confusing ways. These people shaped how you saw yourself and your place in the world.

The emotions they stirred within you—fear, rejection, self-doubt—became part of your subconscious landscape.

I use a process I call the **Primal Tool** (or slide projector method) to help release these patterns. I'll walk you through how to use it in a later chapter.

For now, know this:

You have a reliable way to clear the emotional charge that's been holding you back. With guided visualization, you'll revisit each of these people and gently release what's been stored.

The result is powerful, grounded healing.

✦ Practice with Me: Protect Your Inner Sanctuary

Your energy is sacred.

Not everything deserves access to your inner space.

Not every thought deserves your attention.

You are allowed to choose peace.

✦ *Take a deep breath.*

✦ *Let your body to exhale.*

✦ ***Say~***

"*I protect what is sacred.*"

"*My peace is not up for negotiation.*"

Visualize your energy like a soft glowing light surrounding you–calm, steady, untouchable.

Anything heavy falls away.

Everything sacred remains.

You are separate from whatever energy is surrounding you—you are safe with yourself.'

You carry gifts that protect you–and you'll learn more about them in the chapters ahead.

For now, just rest in this knowing:

You are your own sanctuary.

Chapter 9

Trusting What You Feel

We all carry emotional weight from the past—
old wounds, fears, judgments, and defenses that
helped us survive at one point but now quietly
drains our energy.

These energetic patterns don't just live in the
mind; they take root in the body, the nervous
system, and the subtle field around us.

Some of these patterns began in childhood.
Maybe we took on the role of peacemaker,
caretaker, perfectionist, or overachiever. Maybe
we were sensitive souls who felt unsafe,
misunderstood, or even bullied—trying to find a
way to feel safer and more loved.

We absorbed beliefs about ourselves—like "I'm not enough," or "I have to work hard to be accepted"—and unconsciously shaped our lives around those thoughts.

The emotions of others—their expectations, moods, and needs—can shape us in ways we don't even realize. These habits become so familiar that we stop questioning them.

We might have learned to silence our needs, dim our light, or carry the emotional weight of others. These habits can be so familiar we don't even question them.

But when we begin to wake up spiritually, these old patterns start to feel heavy. You might notice that something you used to tolerate—an unhealthy dynamic, a draining job, a cluttered home, or a harsh inner voice—suddenly becomes unbearable. That discomfort isn't a failure. It's a sign of growth.

Your soul is asking you to let go of what no longer matches your truth.

Letting go doesn't mean you have to make dramatic changes overnight—it just means that you're ready to stop carrying what no longer fits.

It begins with noticing when something feels tight, heavy, or contracted in your body.

Pause and ask yourself:

✦ *Is this still serving me?*

✦ *Or is it something I've outgrown?*

When you ask that question with sincerity, your intuition will answer. Sometimes it's a whisper. Sometimes it's a knowing in your gut.

You might feel a sense of relief just by acknowledging what's no longer aligned.

Releasing old patterns takes courage. These patterns have kept us safe. Even when they hurt us, they've been our armor. But you don't have to rip them off all at once. You can loosen your grip gently. You can say,

"Thank you for helping me survive. But I don't need you anymore."

Try visualizing yourself placing the old belief or pattern in a ball of light and letting it float away.

Or imagine gently setting it down in a small boat, and watching it drift down the river.

You are allowed to be free.

You are allowed to evolve.

This work isn't about blame—it's about liberation.

It's not about fixing yourself—it's about returning to your essence.

You're not here to carry everyone else's pain, meet everyone's expectations, or shrink yourself to stay safe.

You're here to expand. To come alive. To feel your own spirit moving through you!

Each time you release what no longer serves you, you make more room for what does: joy, clarity, peace, creativity, connection.

Letting go is not a loss.

It's a return—to who you truly are.

✦ Practice With Me: Return to What's True

When the world feels noisy, come back to the quiet within you.

When your thoughts feel loud, remember—you are not your thoughts.

You are the one who observes.

The one who notices.

You are the one who chooses.

✦ *Place your hand on your chest.*

✦ *Feel your breath.*

✦ *Feel your body remembering how to soften.*

✦ **Say~**

"I choose what aligns with love."

"I return to what is true."

"I release what is not mine."

Let this become your quiet reset—anytime, anywhere.

You don't need to force calm and peace.

You only need to stay open—and allow it.

Chapter 10

A New Way to See

"The two most powerful warriors are patience and time."

~Leo Tolstoy

I haven't always had everything I wanted when I wanted it. But I've come to realize that some things unfold with a delay—what Neville

Goddard would call, "a bridge of incidents."

This is the middle place between your desire and the outcome.

It's the in-between—the unfolding.

It's where you're invited to stop obsessing over how your desire will arrive.

Instead, bring your focus back to two things:

What you truly want, and the feeling that comes with it.

Let the feeling take the lead. Imagine how your body would soften…how your energy would expand…how your breath would slow… if it were already yours. It's as if you already have it.

Let yourself live in that sensation—not just the image of the thing, but the felt experience of living it now.

When you choose gratitude in that space, you align with the version of you who knows it's already on the way.

Sometimes this "holding period" between our desire and its fulfillment can show up as unexpected—or even difficult moments.

But often, these moments are the very moments that make the path possible. They rearrange everything behind the scenes.

Even when it feels uncomfortable, the present moment remains the most powerful place to shift your energy.

When you find yourself on that bridge— between where you are and where you're going— don't rush through it. This is your sacred in-between.

It's all part of the transformation, shaping you into the version of yourself who can fully receive what you're asking for.

You're practicing how to create space within, and expand your perception, so you can hold the life aligned with who you're becoming.

Who and what you believe has created the life you see today. And the more you focus more on what you're grateful for, the more of it you naturally attract.

There will always be something you want that hasn't arrived yet—but trust, it comes in time.

Most of the limits we experience are the ones we've unknowingly placed on ourselves.

When you start to see that everything begins to shift.

That thing we want may come or maybe something better will.

It's the same with goals.

Just because you haven't reached one yet, doesn't mean we have failed. Sometimes a goal is there to move you toward something even more meaningful–and you don't realize it until later.

Stay open.

Allow your abundant being to unfold with grace.

Say~

"I am all I need."

*And then **say~***

"I am is who I am and what I create."

Tell yourself,

"I am amazed at who I am and what I am creating. Everything always works out."

Now **feel** how content you are.

Feel your confidence.

This is how you begin creating a new reality.

This awareness—paired with intention and separation from ego— is your beautiful unfolding.

It's your quiet strength.

Your becoming.

With this, you begin living from the version of you who is already aligned with your inner calm—and living the life you came here to live.

Every person can access this with intention and practice.

Mindset Matters—Step Out of the Old and into the New

Your abundant mindset is a practice—

A belief you return to that helps you stay connected to the still, quiet part of your mind. It's the part that doesn't react quickly but sees with clarity and trust.

The present moment can feel like peace—or like pain—but it's always where your power lives.

The moment you realize your current mindset isn't doing your future any favors, you can choose to shift.

Each day becomes a new invitation to stay open and witness your life unfold.

Awareness is the first step to change. It brings clarity—and from that clarity, intention arises.

With intention, you can release what no longer serves you and make space for a new perspective—one that feels lighter, calmer, and no longer trapped in the old patterns of reactivity.

Unforeseen Circumstances Help to Raise Awareness

When life pushes us into darker emotions, it takes true spiritual strength to stay centered.

Trauma—whether from war, psychological wounds, addiction, depression, or harmful patterns—reinforces fear at a deeper level. It takes great courage to stay grounded when you've learned to react from that place.

A spiritual warrior learns to detach from these intensified, limiting beliefs and return to truth, again and again.

This is where focus and devotion are essential. You're learning how to connect with more love from your true self.

When you're grounded in awareness, your mind has more room for what truly matters.

You're learning to detach from the negative, repetitive thoughts—the ones that once shaped limiting beliefs about who you were.

Beliefs that were never true.

Now you're tapping into your intuitive self. The one who creates–not through force–but through blessing.

And from here, there is more space to create what truly matters.

Shifting away from what no longer serves you often begins with a simple thought~

I'm going to try something different.

You can keep the negative charge on the edges by practicing gentle detachment. Aligning with your inner power means choosing to stay on the edges of ego.

You don't react—you observe.

You witness what ego offers without attaching or engaging.

This is how you shift into higher consciousness and align with truth.

Most thoughts are random and fleeting. A thought doesn't become a belief unless we keep repeating it.

It's helpful to remind yourself:

It's only a thought and a thought can be changed.

When you experience a strong or recurring emotion– especially one tied to fear or lack– recognize that it likely stems from a habitual thought pattern.

Thoughts, when repeated, become beliefs. And beliefs begin shaping your life.

So when you notice a familiar thought that drains you, acknowledge it.

Then gently let it pass, like a cloud drifting through the sky. Then, notice the lighter energy that follows, and remind yourself: .

You are not that thought.

This works best for thoughts that aren't deeply rooted.

But if the feeling is heavy or sudden–if it pulls you down and doesn't lift easily—then a quick redirection might not be enough.

That's when you reach for your power release tool. (I'll guide you through how to use this tool in one of the upcoming chapters.) It helps you work beneath the surface—not just shifting the thought, but transforming the belief that feeds it.

It may take a little more time and presence than simply changing your focus, but it's worth it.

Don't let your ego convince you that it's too much effort.

That's just another trick to keep you stuck.

Instead, shift your attention to something peaceful, positive, or divine.

Gaze at that presence.

Let it soften your nervous system.

Let it anchor you.

Feel yourself return to center.

The emotion may feel real—but it doesn't have to define your reality.

Even a small moment—

A tiny shift—can be an invitation to rise.

Change the thought.

Change the belief.

Change your life.

✦ Practice With Me: You Don't Have to Struggle Anymore

You were never meant to earn love through effort.

You weren't meant to feel exhausted.

You don't have to suffer in order to grow.

You are allowed to feel lighter.

✦ *Take a quiet moment.*

✦ *Breathe slowly.*

✦ *Let your nervous system soften.*

✦ *Let your body remember the truth.*

You are safe. You are loved. You are enough.

✦ *Remember who you truly are— beyond the fear,*
   the pressure, and the past.

Say to yourself~

"*I release the struggle.*"

"*I choose grace.*"

"*I allow Life to support me.*"

Even just one breath of permission can change
everything.

PART TWO

Daily Practice & Deeper Awareness

.

Chapter 11

From Stuck to Centered

Energy healing isn't about "doing" more. It's about receiving more.

When you sit down with the intention to allow and receive energy to heal, you are staying open, and you are saying "yes" to your life force.

That's when real change happens.

You shift from control and fear into trust and receptivity. You create a space where healing and insight can flow in.

And it often happens in the quietest moments — when you simply sit down, breathe, and say:

"I accept. I am in agreement with life. I resist nothing."

That's the true receiving mode.

And the universe responds.

Learning to Receive with Grace

Accepting a gift is an act of grace. And yet, many people struggle to receive — often because of pride, conditioning, (the way we're raised), or self-protection. You might not even realize you're resisting until you start paying attention.

Imagine planning the perfect gift for someone you love — you save money, search carefully, wrap it with beauty and intention. You give it to them with joy in your heart, only to have them ignore it, downplay it, or say they can't accept it.

It would be disappointing, right?

That's how divine energy feels when we block its gifts. The universe is always offering — love, guidance, healing, clarity. But if we're too proud, guarded, or distracted to accept what it's trying to offer us, we miss it.

Who This Is For:

This path is absolutely for you if you have ever felt unseen, unheard, or held back by past pain or fear. It's for those who've never known softness or safety in their own hearts.

It's also for the everyday soul—the person who's curious, who feels a flicker inside saying "there's more," even if everything seems fine on the surface. No matter where you start from, you are meant to receive this healing.

Stay open. Be aware. Pay attention to your intuition and ideas that you might not ordinarily take much notice of. Receive what's being offered. It's meant for you.

How Energy Works in the Body

When you receive healing energy, it strengthens your aura — the energetic field around you — creating a buffer from negativity. You might still be sensitive, but you become far less vulnerable.

Energy work helps you stay in your own space.

As the energy flows through your body, it moves up from your feet through all seven chakras. Each energy center is cleansed, balanced, and recharged. This process supports every layer of your being:

✦   Physically: it improves circulation, strengthens the immune system, and supports cellular repair.

✦   Emotionally: it calms the nervous system, lifts anxiety, and stabilizes mood.

✦   Mentally: it clears mental clutter, improves focus, and boosts clarity.

✦   Spiritually: it deepens your connection with your intuition, your spiritual guides, and the divine.

Sometimes it takes several minutes to feel the energy and it will be subtle. Other times it will feel strong. Even if you don't feel dramatic sensations during a session, the healing is still happening. A quiet session is just as powerful as one that feels intense.

Trust that the energy is doing exactly what you need.

How to Tune In with Meditation

Tuning in is the practice of returning to yourself.

It's one of the most powerful ways to start your day.

Even five minutes can make a difference in how you think, feel, and respond.

When you include this practice in the morning–which I highly recommend—it can offer a powerful boost of clarity and awareness—guidance that you might not otherwise receive that day. This presence of energy can be the difference between feeling scattered or grounded.

When I say "tuning in," I mean opening yourself to the divine energy that's already here—surrounding you, waiting to support you. It's allowing yourself to be present with this energy as you sit, ground in stillness, stay quiet, and make the intention to receive.

It's like sinking beneath the surface noise of the mind and dropping into still, sacred waters.

How I Begin

I begin by staying open and I create a receptive space for the energy that is meant for me.

I sit with both feet flat on the ground, close my eyes,

I allow the thoughts of the day to arise.

I let them surface without judgment–gently acknowledging them, and then letting them pass.

When I begin to shift into a more neutral and centered state, I bring my awareness to the point between my eyebrows—the third eye. I rest there for a moment, allowing my energy to settle and then observe in my mind's eye the energy surrounding my head area, usually higher.

Then I stay open and receptive. Often, I sense a subtle light or energetic presence just to the left of my head. That's when I know I'm ready to shift from the mental noise into stillness.

I don't try to force anything—I simply allow and receive. It's where I connect and then relax and receive, and if my mind wanders, I guide myself back to the lighter energy a bit higher than my head.

I do this meditation so naturally now, it feels effortless—like second nature. I hardly have to even think about it. I know the energy is flowing naturally through each of the seven chakra centers, gently cleansing, opening, and restoring balance as it rises.

I don't try to figure out what the energy is doing. I have learned to trust. Sometimes I can feel it's working on me physically, where I can feel it in different chakras and areas of the body, and other times it's giving more clarity.

Each person has a unique experience. What one person feels or heals through may look very different for someone else—whether in the sensations they feel or how fast they heal. Everyone's journey is private and personal.

Energy enters through the feet, but it also flows in through seventh portal at the posterior area of the head. As this current moves through the brain, it often settles near the cerebellum, supporting clarity, brain health, emotional regulation, and intuition.

As your clarity and intuition sharpen, your connection to your soul self strengthens.

Ordinarily, the cerebellum controls movement, balance, and posture, as well as cognitive and emotional stability. When you first begin receiving energy, you might feel a brief sense of vertigo—a sign that your vestibular system and brain are responding to the flow.

The energy travels upward from beneath the ground, entering through the feet and moving toward the base of the spine, where the first energy center— the root chakra is located. The root chakra represents grounding, safety, and survival. When it's blocked, you may feel anxious or unstable.

When it's open and energized, we feel rooted, supported by life, and confident in our ability to meet our basic needs.

The second chakra, the sacral chakra, governs our creativity, sexuality, and flow. It's located just below the navel. Energy that becomes clear and free there clears stagnation and restores our ability to feel creative vitality.

The third chakra, the heart chakra, is the bridge between body and spirit. It governs love, compassion, and forgiveness. As the energy rises through the heart, it softens old wounds and expands our capacity to love—both ourselves and others—with authenticity and grace.

The fifth chakra, the throat chakra, is our center of communication, truth, and self-expression. When this center opens, we find our voice–not just to speak, but to live in alignment with who we really are. We begin to express our truth clearly, without fear or distortion.

The sixth chakra, the third eye, located between the eyebrows, governs intuition, inner sight and spiritual awareness. As energy flows through this center, it quiets the mental noise and sharpens our ability to perceive subtle truths. We begin to see through illusion and connect to deeper wisdom.

The seventh chakra, the crown chakra, at the top of the head, is our connection to the divine, our soul, and the infinite. This is the portal through which our soul enters the body at birth, and through which it leaves at death. When this center opens, we feel a profound sense of peace, unity, and spiritual connection—as if we are part of something far greater than ourselves.

Energy moving through these centers doesn't just cleanse—it activates, lifts, awakens. As I receive energy more consistently, I feel myself becoming lighter, more expanded, and with more clarity.

Sometimes, I feel intense warmth at the center of one or both feet—an energizing, revitalizing sensation. Other times, it's more subtle, a soft, gentle awareness in the soles, or a light sensation in another part of my body. I also like to notice areas of discomfort or sensitivity, especially in my neck, shoulders, or mid-back and I keep bringing my awareness there until it dissipates and I feel lighter.

If I pay attention, I can feel a light pressure or subtle sensation in one of my chakras—most often in my third chakra, the solar plexus. It's like a soft activation of presence, reminding me that energy is moving or something is coming into balance.

As I write this, I can feel energy in my throat chakra—the center of communication. Sometimes I hear a few words or phrases of gentle guidance; other times, there's silence. Even when nothing seems to be happening outwardly, I know the energy is cleansing and nourishing. My chakra system supports me physically, emotionally, and energetically.

After this, with my eyes closed, I bring my focus to a state of quiet awareness. I shift back to the mind — and often find that it feels lighter, clearer, and more open. This is a sacred moment for me— calm, grounded, and protected.

I often sit like this for five or ten minutes in the morning (or more, when time allows). I simply allow the energy to move through me.

✦ Practice With Me: Return to Stillness & Light

✦ *Start by sitting quietly with your feet on the floor. Breathe. Let your attention shift from your breath to the subtle energy around you.*

✦ *You may feel a soft, light presence just above or beside your head.*

✦ *Allow yourself to receive—without effort or pressure.*

✦ *You may not feel anything. It took me a long while before I could sense anything clearly when I tuned in.*

You don't have to feel or visualize anything. Just stay open.

✦ *Do what feels right for you and if you have a visualization, that's a gift for you, and if you sense or feel lightness or energy, that's lovely too—but not necessary.*

✦ *Just stay open.*

✦ *Now, gently notice how your solar plexus feels— your third chakra.*

✦ *If it feels heavy or tight, bring your focus there and breathe into it.*

✦ *Over time, it will shift — becoming lighter and freer.*

✦ *This chakra is your power center, and when it's clear, you feel grounded, confident, and calm.*

When You're Ready for Deeper Energy Healing

When you're ready for a deeper energy healing—where you are calling in energy more deliberately for stronger physical or emotional restoration, you might notice stronger sensations of energy—sometimes centered in the third chakra, the solar plexus, or the third eye, and even in your hands. Many people feel it in their palms, especially if they've done healing work before. The soles of your feet may feel hotter, more centered, comforting. You might feel it in your palms during prayer.

Sometimes, I visualize a soft white effervescent healing pillar of light moving through me—beginning from beneath the ground, rising through the soles of my feet, flowing through my entire energy body. I don't need to direct it. I simply imagine it to be strong, intentional, and yet incredibly soft and soothing.

At times, when I focus on the third chakra, I can feel the heavier energy I've picked up throughout the day begin to release. I stay with it until the energy clears, and the center feels light again.

I often hear a very soft ringing in my ears after about five or ten minutes. Other times, the sensations are more subtle.

But remember—whatever you feel (or don't feel) is not a measure of how much healing you are receiving.

Even if you are having an energy session that feels quite boring, you are still receiving deep healing. Sometimes the shifts happen beneath the surface.

What matters most is how you'll feel afterwards: clearer, lighter, and more energized.

Energy Healing Work Moves You Along Faster

Energy healing moves more easily when you work with intention—when you go with the flow rather than reacting or resisting. Healing happens when you tune in consciously and say,

"I accept." or "I am in agreement with life."

What It Feels Like When I'm Out of Alignment

When I drift out of alignment, I feel it—my energy becomes stagnant, my heart feels closed, my body tenses, and I lost my natural sense of flow.

At first, it might show up as frustration, overwhelm, or fatigue. Then I notice myself looping the same thoughts without clarity. I become more anxious and doubtful.

That's why I return to this cleansing practice regularly, not just to feel better but to stay connected to who I really am.

Throughout the week, I try to return to this state in small, simple ways—gratitude for a moment of connection. I notice the beauty in someone's heart, or the quiet sound of leaves in the wind, or even a few seconds of stillness and peace.

Clearing my chakras helps me soften and realign. I move through the world from a grounded, open, and attuned place. I don't just function better, I feel like myself again.

As you tune in more often, you may begin to feel a new kind of calm and physical healing. Imagine uncovering a soft, invisible shield around you—one rooted in love protecting your energy.

You begin to realize it's there because you are already protected. You start to trust yourself more.

You want to share that love, not from depletion, but from overflow. This is your sacred space.

This is where you are safe, and where you are well.

Your process doesn't have to be perfect or complicated. It's simple. Begin by sitting and receiving. Let the energy work on your behalf. Rest. The tools, the gifts, the clarity — they'll unfold as you go.

✦ Practice With Me: Receiving Energy, Reclaiming Calm

✦ *Find a quiet space where you won't be disturbed. Sit comfortably with your feet flat on the floor and your hands resting gently in your lap with palms gently facing up, or over your heart.*

✦ *Close your eyes, and let your breath begin to soften. There's nothing to do here—just be.*

✦ Take a moment to feel your body. Feel the weight of your hips grounding you.

✦ Feel your spine rising gently, supported by the earth below and the sky above.

✦ Let yourself drop into presence.

✦ Now, begin to imagine energy gently rising from beneath the ground—soft, warm, and golden. It moves through the soles of your feet and up through your legs, to your first root chakra, bringing with it healing, stability, and calm.

✦ Let it move slowly, with ease.

✦ Let it rise.

✦ As this energy travels through your body, notice any sensation—warmth, tingling, or stillness. If you feel nothing at all, that's okay too.

Energy works beneath the surface. Trust it.

✦ Let this energy move to any area that needs healing. Breathe into it. With every breath, invite more clarity, more softness, more of your own inner light.

✦ Now imagine a shield of light forming gently around you–not a wall, but a loving, protective boundary.

This shield is made of energy that loves you.

It filters what comes in and what goes out.

You are safe here.

✦ Feel the calm that begins to settle. The kind of calm that isn't dependent on outside circumstances. A calm that is yours.

✦ Now tune into your heart. From this place of safety and connection, let love begin to rise–not from effort, but from overflow.

You don't need to give from depletion anymore.

You are allowed to feel full first.

This is your sacred space.

You are protected here.

You are clear.

You are calm.

You are well.

✦ *When you're ready, gently bring your awareness back to your breath.*

✦ *Wiggle your fingers and toes.*

✦ *Open your eyes softly, and carry this calm with you into the rest of your day.*

Choosing Calm in the Middle of a Hard Moment

At times throughout the day when I get upset or distracted with something, I use a practical tool, one that I call a "release tool" that helps me gently disconnect from the low vibration energy of a person, place, or situation. You'll learn how to use it soon—I'll walk you through it.

Other times, I simply stay aware of what's bothering me—and I observe it for a few seconds as it begins to drift away—then I gently shift my focus to a peaceful, divine image. This process takes only three to five seconds to use and can be done anytime, anywhere. As you continue using this softening practice, it naturally becomes part of your inner routine— and it often helps more than you would expect.

✦ **Practice With Me: Release**

✦ *Close your eyes.*

✦ *Bring to mind a person, thought, or feeling that you're ready to release.*

You don't need to fix it.

You don't need to fully understand it.

You are just making the decision right now to release.

Say~`

" I am ready to release."

"I trust the process."

Chapter 12

More About How the Energy Works for You

Each time you quiet the mind and sit in stillness, you begin to reconnect with your body, breath, and subtle energy. As you breathe with awareness, you may notice sensations in your energy centers, your chakras, gently awakening. This energy is intelligent and healing. It flows upward through your entire energetic system.

With continued practice, this flow strengthens your spiritual alignment, revitalizes your energy field, and clears emotional stagnation. It supports the physical body too—increasing circulation, boosting the immune system, encouraging cellular repair, and calming the nervous system. You may notice your pulse slow, your breath deepen, and your stress dissolve.

Over time, your inner awareness sharpens. You feel more present, more emotionally resilient, and more connected to your higher intuition.

You may even begin to sense loving communication from a spiritual guide–or simply feel more deeply guided from within. Energy work doesn't just bring balance—it brings you home to yourself.

Starting Out with a Visualization

Visualization is what you see with your intention–a way of connecting to your deeper consciousness. With your eyes closed and your awareness tuned inward, you might find yourself in a spiritual setting—a quiet room, an open field with flowers, a lush damp forest, a sacred temple, or any place that brings deep peace.

These images will vary from person to person, and they will show up without being forced.

They carry healing, wonder, or a sense of deep protection. This is one way your deeper consciousness speaks to you.

Sometimes, visualization brings a glimpse of a memory—not just a thought, but a feeling that moves something deep within you. One of these memories for me is from childhood. After spending 18 months living in a large, dark, 200-year-old house in Germany—a place that carried heavy, unsettled energy—I remember the moment I stepped off a plane in Spain.

The contrast was immediate and overwhelming. The lightness in the air, the warmth of the sun, the sight of orange trees all around me–it felt like joy itself had wrapped around me. It wasn't just a beautiful place, it felt mystical. As if I had stepped into the version of life I was always meant to feel.

I also had the memory that shaped my understanding of peace that came from the near-death experience I had at six years old. I remember the love–the absolute sense of being home. That moment never left me–and it still reminds me that this deeper feeling is always there for me to reconnect with it.

Now when I feel stress, or tension, or even tediousness of moments in the day, I take a few seconds to a minute to reconnect with that higher energy. I close my eyes, breathe, visualize, and feel the peace that lives beneath everything.

You can do this too. You can grasp that feeling that you once had even if it lasted only a few seconds in your life. A fleeting moment of joy, freedom, or lightness you thought was lost. When you tune in and stay open, you can relive it.

And if you're able to re-live it, you can re-create it.

Use your imagination to tap into your best feeling memory or moment–because your imagination is not pretend. It's a bridge to something real. It is the meeting place between you and the sacred mysteries of your soul. It reaches far deeper than we realize.

That's the power of conscious connection. If a memory doesn't come to mind, simply picture something that brings up the feeling you're reaching for.

Remember this:

Your inner light is always stronger than our darkest shadow.

Healing doesn't come from effort alone—it comes from presence, intention, and more inner openness.

Because we are spiritual beings having a human experience, we can return to that truth anytime we choose. Sometimes meditation can feel mundane, but don't forget, it can also bring surprising moments of insight and wonder. You are connecting to the Divine—to receive guidance and support that's always been with you.

You can connect with a sacred presence, what many experience as their *guardian angel*, always near, always protective, even when you're not aware of it. As your awareness grows, you may begin to sense this presence more clearly. You can ask for guidance anytime.

They are always listening. Always available. Always supporting you.

How to Discern Between Your Angel and a Negative Entity

As your sensitivity increases and your awareness deepens, it's natural to begin sensing different types of energy. Many people connect with a sacred presence they experience as a guardian angel—a loving protective force that offers comfort and guidance.

But staying open also means becoming more receptive to all kinds of energy, especially in the early stages of your spiritual practice. This is why it's essential to set a clear intention to remain aligned only with energies that are supportive, positive, and divine. You can stay open while also firmly closing the door to anything that does not serve your highest good.

There is a distinct difference between an angel or guide– who is an extension of the Divine— and an entity that feels heavier, manipulative, or draining. Negative entities may offer details, probabilities, or bits of information that feel accurate at first, but over time their influence can become confusing, disempowering, or energetically depleting.

Some people who channel or receive intuitive messages don't always filter what they allow in, which can unintentionally open the door to unhelpful or manipulative energies.

While this isn't something to fear, it's important to acknowledge—especially for those who've experienced it. Clear intention, energetic boundaries, and discernment are essential parts of any spiritual practice.

The power of your attention helps you stay aligned with higher frequencies, but true discernment comes from being grounded, centered, and willing to notice what genuinely resonates, and what does not.

The key to knowing the difference lies in how the energy feels in your heart. A true guide will bring a sense of peace, clarity, and gentle strength—never fear, urgency, or emotional instability.

When you're centered in your intention and grounded in love, your inner clarity becomes your protection.

Tuning in for Different Purposes

Sometimes, especially when you're just beginning to meditate or tune in, it can feel difficult to connect with the feeling or visualization you're hoping for. You might find yourself trying too hard, but the truth is, there's no need to force anything or follow a specific method.

You don't even have to visualize. Many times I don't even think about it much at all. I simply stay aware of what's happening around and within me, and that's enough. Other times, I do use visualizations more intentionally—especially when I have a goal that I'm working towards and I want to stay energetically aligned with it. I also used to visualize more often when I felt depleted or hopeless, as a way to reconnect with the joy of my own truth—who I knew I was deep down, and how I knew I could feel all the time.

I keep it simple. I tune in for different purposes depending on what I need. In the morning, I receive energy to help with physical vitality and clarity. Other times, I stay open to receive healing energy to unblock and revitalize my chakras, or to stay aligned with guidance.

To be honest, I don't usually try to figure out what the energy is doing. I just allow it, trusting that it's giving me exactly what I need in that moment.

Most times I tune in with clear intention is when I'm feeling upset or unwell and want to shift into a better state. In those moments, I open to receive energy, and I hear quiet guidance, reassurance, or fresh insight. Other times, I sense a gentle invitation—a whisper from the stillness within, nudging me toward clarity and alignment and even a new perspective.

If you're not able to tune in consistently, try experimenting. Skip your practice for a few days, then take time to meditate–either in the morning or at night, and notice the difference.

Pay attention to your energy, awareness, and clarity afterward. How does it compare to the days you didn't tune in? After your next meditation, observe how you feel over the following few hours. You might be surprised by the shift.

You can begin by staying gently aware throughout the day, especially when you remember to check in with yourself. Notice how your solar plexus—the third energy center–feels. This chakra acts as a receiver, taking in the energy around you.

If you're someone who naturally gives energy to others, you may also sense energy moving outward from your solar plexus. This can be more subtle to detect, unless you're highly attuned to how energy settles and shifts within and around you.

When you're around negativity, you might feel a heaviness or pressure–the third energy center. This feeling often goes unnoticed unless you're consciously staying open and aware of your body's signals.

*If you'd like to practice sensing what your third
chakra is holding, try this—*

The next time you're in a difficult or negative
situation gently bring your attention to your
solar plexus and observe how it feels. You may
not sense much at first, but with practice, you'll
begin to notice how external energy affects your
body. After tuning in or meditating, this area
will often feel lighter, more open and balanced.

If you're feeling the presence of heavy or dense
energy—remember that you have the power to
diffuse it. Focus on your third eye and feel it
gently open. As you do, the energy from this
center can strengthen and begin to clear the
space around you.

Even a few seconds of focused awareness is
enough to keep it activated. With practice, this
becomes more natural. I'll explain more about
how to access and work with this gift in a later
chapter.

At the same time, it's also worth questioning how often you are exposed to energy that doesn't serve you. If you notice a consistent heaviness in a particular area of your life, it may be time to reflect on whether that environment truly supports your well-being. Sometimes it's not just about managing energy, but about recognizing when it's time to set a firmer boundary—or even step away entirely.

"With awareness, reality shifts."

~Don Miguel Ruiz

True change doesn't come from waiting for the outside world to shift—it comes from the quiet decision to do something different. I remember reaching a turning point in my early twenties when I realized something had to give. I was chasing answers but feeling more lost by the day.

Deep down, I knew I couldn't keep going the way I was. Fear had quietly shaped so many of my choices, especially in childhood. I often longed to try things but held back, unsure of myself.

One fear in particular stayed with me for years: water. I was terrified of water the first five years of my life. Throughout my childhood, I had recurring dreams of drowning in the ocean with others around me–always feeling helpless, and pulled under. It took time to release that fear, but it taught me something important: healing doesn't always come quickly, but it begins the moment we choose to stop running.

At one point in my life, I had a close group of friends who were professional scuba divers. They would often ask me to join them, and it looked like it could be an incredible experience. I wanted to join them, but I couldn't get past the claustrophobia I imagined I'd feel underwater with all the gear. I decided it was something I would have to pass up on.

Ten years later, after traveling more and snorkeling in the ocean, something shifted. I realized I wanted to face the fear and try diving. I enrolled in a class, earned my scuba certification, and planned my first open-water dive on a trip to the St. Martinique Island in the Caribbean. The moment I descended into the water and experienced the wonders of the deep, I was hooked.

During that trip, I was given the option to do a dive through a cave, but I honored my boundaries, and declined. I didn't need to prove anything, not even to myself.

It doesn't matter how old you are or what your circumstances look like—your joy is still waiting for you. Approach each day like a gentle treasure hunt.

It may be baby steps at times, but as you use your tools and trust the process, you'll grow, change and create what you truly believe in.

✦ Practice With Me: Trust What You're Becoming

Say~

"I trust to accept what is waiting for me to receive." Let that be your compass—not fear, not doubt.

Allow a quiet trust in the unfolding.

Chapter 13

Opening to Energy: A Gentle Guide to Receiving Spiritual Support

Your Intention Is What Matters Most

When you tune in with love, clarity, and the desire to grow, you connect to a higher intuition. You can choose to listen to your own intuition, or open to the presence of a spiritual guide—a gentle, loving energy that helps protect, uplift, and support you.

It might feel like your guardian angel or a wise, peaceful presence holding space for you. However it appears, the feeling is unmistakable, as if you're being held by something greater than yourself. Trust that when your intuition is rooted in love, you'll always be guided.

Trust Your Anchor

The more you trust yourself, the more clearly you'll sense what's true. Fear creates static–it pulls you out of your inner knowing. But when your heart is open, you can feel your way home every time. Even in moments of doubt, your anchor is within you.

Let the following *Practice With Me* session guide you back to that calm, steady center within.

✦ Practice With Me: Feeling the Presence of Divine Guidance

✦ *Take a moment to sit in stillness.*

✦ *Let your body soften and your breath slow.*

✦ *As your awareness settles, gently place your attention in your heart space.*

✦ *You can place a hand there if it helps.*

✦ *Now invite your highest self—the part of you that is always connected to truth—to come forward.*

Breathe into that connection.

✦ *In your mind or out loud,* **speak this intention~**

"I choose to connect only with divine love and guidance."

"I welcome only what is for my highest good."

Feel the energy around you begin to soften, lift, or warm—even in the subtlest of ways.

That subtle feeling is your guidance beginning to meet you.

You may notice a sense of peace, openness, or quiet knowing.

You might feel nothing at all, and that's okay too. The connection is still there.

Remember, you are still learning how to sense energy and this takes practice.

Now ask inwardly~

What does truth feel like in my body?

Let your system show you. Maybe it's a steadiness in your chest, a quiet joy, or a clear path. This is how your soul says yes.

If you're ever unsure, return to this space. Your heart knows.

Divine guidance never pressures, never confuses, and never drains. It feels like love, steady, kind, and aligned with who you truly are.

Building Your Daily Ritual

Your energy practice doesn't have to be long or elaborate. Even two minutes of tuning in can shift your

Try this~

+ Find a quiet space. Sit with your feet grounded.

+ Take a few deep breaths and close your eyes.

+ Open your awareness to the energy above and around you.

+ Stay in stillness and simply receive.

+ If you have more time, allow energy to move through each chakra.

+ Visualize or sense the energy cleansing, balancing, and energizing each center.

+ You can also set intentions — for healing, for clarity, for peace.

+ Pay attention to how you feel after.

+ Do you notice more energy, calm, or joy?

+ Do you feel more in tune with yourself?

Use these quiet moments to reconnect with the divine.

You are never alone in this work.

Closing Reflections on Trust and Growth

We are spiritual beings living a human experience. The tools we use — meditation, energy healing, visualization, our gifts, intention — are ways of remembering who we really are.

You don't need to be perfect.

You don't have to get it "right."

You just need to show up — open, honest, and willing.

The energy will meet you there.

Some days will feel magical. Others will feel quiet or even dull. But even in the stillness, you are being transformed.

Let your spiritual practice be a treasure hunt — not a chore.

Each moment of awareness is a seed. Each breath, an offering.

Each time you say yes to love, clarity, and healing, you move yourself forward on the path.

You are shifting now. And everything beautiful you desire is already within you.

✦ Practice With Me: Strengthen Your Energy Field

Healing energy doesn't just shift your thoughts, it strengthens your field.

Every time you return to stillness, your aura grows clearer and stronger.

Each time you choose calm, you reinforce the buffer between your energy and the world.

This is how you can stop absorbing everything around how.

This is how you stay in your own sacred space.

✦ *Take a few slow breaths.*

✦ *Imagine a gentle light forming around your body and expanding out slowly—soft, but powerful.*

✦ *This is your aura, your energy field, your spiritual boundary.*

Say~

"I stay rooted in my own vibration."

"I am protected by light."

"My energy field is clear and strong."

Feel into that space.

You don't have to block or resist anything—just remain centered and sovereign.

You are far less "pullable" now.

You are not here to carry what isn't yours.

Chapter 14

The Primal Tool–A Step-by-Step Guide for Deep Release

This is the foundational tool I teach for releasing energy at the subconscious level—where most emotional patterns and limiting beliefs dwell.

I call it the primal tool because it reaches deeper than surface thoughts or reactions. It reaches the root where unconscious heaviness, old pain, and ingrained negativity often reside.

Before using any of the other tools in this book, I encourage you to start with this one regularly. The amount of time you'll need to use it varies from person to person, but when practiced consistently for a few weeks to a couple of months, it tends to be most powerful.

You'll know when you're done—you'll feel lighter, clearer, and something inside you will just feel different.

Think of this tool as a way to clear the static from your inner field, a way to create space that helps the mind quiet and the energy body soften.

When you begin here, other practices, like affirmations, release work, visualizations, or boundary setting, become much more effective. They're no longer working against buried resistance, but flowing through a clearer, more receptive space.

This tool only needs to be used at the beginning of your process—you don't have to repeat it constantly. It gently unwinds layers you may not even realize you're carrying.

Over time, it helps you release what doesn't belong—old programming, self-criticism, inherited fear—and come back to your own truth.

For me, this tool was a lifeline. I was so grateful to feel the heavy waves of self-doubt, fear, and resentment slowly begin to lift. After using the tool daily with five different people, I felt lighter—more free. It felt liberating to realize I could finally separate myself from toxic energy I was never meant to carry.

How to Use the Primal Tool

The Primal Tool works by helping you release the emotional charge that formed in early relationships in the early formative years of your childhood, the kind of charge that shaped your sense of self and your place in the world.

As you begin this practice, you'll choose three to five people from those early years—individuals who triggered fear, rejection, shame, or self-doubt at a core level.

These relationships may have been confusing, painful, or simply emotionally charged. The purpose isn't to revisit the pain, but to clear the energy that still lingers in your field. This tool allows you to release those patterns at the

subconscious level—where they were formed—
so you can move forward feeling lighter, freer,
and more rooted in your true self.

When I used this tool, I began by focusing on the
faces or energetic essence of a few people who
caused confusion, fear, or emotional discomfort.
I couldn't fully name the emotions I felt, but I
was able to release anyways.

I gazed at their face for a few moments, allowing
the image to stay present long enough until it
began to shift. As you continue to look, you
aren't focusing on the feeling—only observing
the face—and gently allowing release to happen.

Sometimes it faded slowly, other times it started
to shake or vibrate slightly before moving
backward and disappearing altogether.

Afterward, I checked in with my solar plexus
(my third chakra), and it almost always felt
lighter–no longer as heavy as before. I would

scan upward through my heart to my mind, and there would be a sense of calm.

Once that energy cleared, I shifted to an image of something divine and beautiful—a visual reset that brought my energy back to love. After that, I moved on to the next person, like flipping a slide in a projector.

With each image, I allowed myself to rest in whatever I received first—the shape of their features, the hue of their essence, the subtle energy behind the form. Some faces shifted quickly, others hovered longer.

Each slide held its own story. Some felt light, some heavier. Every time I encountered resistance or heaviness, I paused and returned to the divine image as a reset. I let my awareness breathe there, until calm returned and I felt moved to continue.

I repeated the process with five individuals, one at a time, until each face had softened and diffused. There were times I couldn't see the face clearly—as if I'd forgotten exactly what they looked like. In these moments I shifted my focus to their essence. That was enough.

When I checked in with my energy again, I knew that I had gradually released a deeper layer of negativity—and that it would continue to release over time.

I used this tool twice a day at first, then once daily for a couple of months. Eventually, I noticed something shift: when I brought a person's face into focus, it would fade almost instantly — within five or ten seconds. That's when I knew the tool was really working: the energy was no longer stuck, and I had let it go.

As I continued the process, I noticed that the deep resentment I once carried toward certain people began to soften. I even found myself feeling more neutral, sometimes even peaceful.

Letting go felt like becoming more of the me I wanted to be. It was a quiet relief—like finally setting down a weight I didn't know I'd been carrying.

A Step-by-Step Guide

Begin by using this tool as a foundation to release the weight of your subconscious mind so you maximize the effectiveness of your daily tools. You don't need to use it for more than a few months at most.

When I used it, it took me about a month—practicing a few times a day. If you use it less often, (say, once a week), you'll likely need to practice for a longer period of time.

When you're done, you'll just *know*, and then you can transition into using your everyday practical tools as needed.

How Do I Use the Primal Tool?

You release by focusing on one person at a time.

✦   Step 1: Think of 3 to 7 people who you reacted to in your early years as a child. You don't need to analyze or understand them. Sometimes you'll just sense you're holding something heavy— resentment, self-doubt, fear–or even deeper waves of anger or rage. This feeling may show up in your body, your mood, your energy, or how you react.

✦   Step 2: You may be releasing unconscious pain at the root level with this process. You're not trying to feel or dissect your emotions—you are observing and releasing them through focused intention.

✦   Step 3: One at a time, bring your attention to a person's face—hold both the form and their essence. Watch until the image fades, vibrates, or moves away. Sometimes the image will do all three; other times it might simply fade or dissolve.

✦   Step 4: Over time, this process becomes faster and more natural as you free the subconscious of lower-frequency emotions like resentment, anger, guilt, and shame.

The goal is not to feel or analyze your emotions, but to detach; to observe and release them through focused intention.

Repeat the process with each person until you feel emotionally detached and free.

Why This Works

This tool releases emotions stored at the subconscious level. With repeated use, you reduce the ego's grip and expand your awareness.

Eventually, you stop being triggered by these people or the thoughts connected to them. You feel lighter, more spacious, and more clear.

You Are a Conscious Creator

We're always being called to make a choice—
between the fear-based thoughts of the ego and
the aligned vision of the soul.

Your power lies in how you respond. We can
always recreate each moment— we can shift our
alignment.

Say, *"I'm a vibrational match to all that I desire."*

With every intentional thought, you become
more aligned, more free, and more deeply
connected to your true creative power.

Slipping Backward, Then Rising Higher

Sometimes we regress. That's part of being human. But even in those moments, we are learning something new.

When you catch yourself entertaining an old thought or emotion, meet it with compassion.

Then pause, and choose again.

Your most enlightened insights often come right after a slip. Let that slip remind you that you're growing in new directions.

Each time you tune in, release, and realign—you become more whole. More free. More you.

✦ Practice With Me: Let Go With Intention

Energy responds to intention, not effort.

The more clearly you choose to release what's no longer aligned, the more space you create for healing and clarity.

You don't need to carry everything. You only need to let go—on purpose.

Close your eyes.

Say~

"I bless it and let go."

"I call my energy back to me."

Check inward. Do you feel lighter, clearer, or more centered?

Even if you don't feel anything right away— trust that the shift is happening.

Chapter 15

Every Day Practical Tools to Support Your Energy

Once you've released the deeper emotional weight from your subconscious using the primal tool, your everyday practices become more effective.

The following tools help shift your mindset in the moment—especially when you feel more triggered, anxious, confused, or overwhelmed.

This practice is not about denying emotion. It's about using one of the practical tools to release the excess charge — the ego's distorted grip — so instead of feeling inner chaos or discomfort, you can respond from truth and peace.

They are especially powerful when you:

+ Feel fear, resentment, or anger toward someone—or even a sense of dread about connecting with a person or group.

+ Can't stop replaying a thought or memory.

+ Want to reset and return to your empowered state.

+ If you suddenly feel heavy, depressed, or insecure after being in a group setting, a crowded place, or a charged environment — even somewhere as ordinary as the grocery store.

Now, let's look at how you can recognize and start using these tools in your everyday life.

How to Recognize an Ego Thought

Not every uncomfortable thought is from the ego, but here's how to tell:

Maybe you were feeling fine, and suddenly your mood dropped.

216

✦	You're looping on a thought and can't seem to stop.

✦	You feel fear, anger, jealousy, or unworthiness out of nowhere

✦	You're obsessing over what someone said, did, or might think.

If you feel any low or uneasy feeling arise for no clear reason; or if you're unsure, use your tool to release the thought and the energy beneath it.

What the Release Tool Is

You're not just releasing the thought itself, but the energy that's been fueling it.

If the feeling clears, it was likely coming from the ego. If not, you've lost nothing.

The more you practice, the more quickly you'll be able to recognize when your mind is caught in these repeating patterns—and more often than not, a release will bring immediate relief.

Tool 1: Releasing Energetic Ties to a Person

Sometimes a person rubs you the wrong way. Other times, it's someone close to you — someone you love but have built up tension or resentment toward. Use this tool to clear the energy and reconnect to truth.

Step-by-Step:

1. Close your eyes and bring the person's face into your awareness.

2. Gaze at their face gently—without judgment or stories. Just observe.

3. Continue until their image fades, vibrates, or moves away.

4. After the release, shift your focus to something loving or calming—a peaceful scene, a symbol of light, or a sense of stillness.

5. You'll feel lighter, more neutral, and more open-hearted around this person.

6. Emotions like fear, resentment, or low self-worth will begin to dissolve, and you'll find yourself feeling more neutral and grounded when interacting with this person.

This tool works whether you're sitting in meditation or standing in line at the store.

Eventually, you'll be able to do it with your eyes open, or even in the middle of a conversation.

Tool 2: Releasing Energy You've Absorbed from a Group Setting

When you've been in a group and feel drained, irritated, or off-center afterward, it may be from absorbing collective energy. Use this simple practice to cleanse your field.

Step-by-Step:

1. Close your eyes and bring the group or crowd into your awareness.

2. Scan the group visually in your mind's eye.

3. Silently say, "Meditate on all."

4. Take your time and watch the crowd fade, vibrate, or move away.

5. Afterward, shift your focus to something peaceful or uplifting.

This restores your aura, clears residual energy, and resets your mood.

Tool 3: Freeing Yourself From Energetic Obsession

Material desires can become obsessive when the wanting begins to feel heavy, anxious, or consuming. This tool helps you return to balance.

It's not about denying your desires, but freeing yourself from the energy of fixation so you can reconnect with peace and clarity.

Step-by-Step:

1. Bring the object of your obsession into your awareness—the thing you've been fixated on or craving, even if it feels out of reach.

2. Gaze at it neutrally. You may feel a pull, craving, or fixation.

3. Allow the energy to fade, shift, or move away.

4. Afterward, shift to a vision of something beautiful or divine— or even a sense of gratitude, peace, or trust.

This doesn't mean you can't want nice things. It just helps you release the attachment or illusion that your happiness depends on having them.

Say,

"I honor the beauty in my life, but I do not cling. I enjoy what's here with gratitude, and I trust the flow when it's time to release. Nothing truly mine can ever be lost."

Tool 4: Releasing an Ego Thought and Emotion

Our thoughts and emotions are powerful forces—they can either connect us to peace of pull us away from it.

The ego often disrupts our peace through the stories and emotions it tells us—to create confusion, guilt, or self-doubt with thoughts of fear usually that can feel so personal and convincing.

This tool offers a way out. It helps you recognize those patterns as energy rather than truth, and gives you a way to clear the charge that activates them.

 With each release, you loosen the ego's hold and return to your natural state of calm awareness.

Step-by-Step:

1. Tune into how you feel. Trace the emotion to the thought that triggered it.

2. Name the thought and feeling clearly.

Example:

"This situation is impossible because of this thing or this person," or

"A situation or a person that needs to change in order for me to be happy."

3. Speak directly to ego. Use this release statement:

"Ego, take the thought that (state the exact thought) and the feeling of (name the emotion), and **RELEASE**."

4. As you say **"RELEASE"** or **"MOVE OFF"**, watch the thought and feeling leave. You may feel a subtle shift or physical sensation.

5. If it lingers, repeat with more detail.

6. Afterward, focus on something divine — a truth, a vision, or something that affirms your light.

Examples:

✦ "Ego, take the thought that I'm a terrible at how I did this wrong, (and name it), and the feeling of self-doubt and low self-worth, and

RELEASE."

or:

✦: "Ego, take the thought that I'm fat when I look in the mirror and the thought of not being enough, and feeling of self-doubt, (and whatever other feelings you have), and

RELEASE."

This practice gets easier and more automatic over time. In the beginning, you may need to repeat it several times a day—but eventually, you'll begin to shift more effortlessly.

Use this tool with any thought that brings you down—especially when it's tied to a heavy emotion. Those loops are not your truth.

Quick Connection to Light and Love

You don't always need a full release process.

Sometimes, all it takes is a moment of tuning in—

+ *Breathe deeply* **and say~**

+ *"I am safe. I am connected to light."*

+ *"I stay open to grace and ease. I allow life to support me."*

✦ *Visualize a place or feeling that connects you to your essence — where your spirit feels alive and free.*

✦ *Let yourself receive the energy of that feeling, even for a few seconds.*

There are moments throughout the day, while driving, walking, or resting—I sometimes visualize the same light I see during meditation. Reconnecting with that sacred feeling, even for a moment, can completely shift my energy and the tone of the day.

Closing Thoughts: You're Becoming a Master of the Shift

These tools are meant to serve your expansion — not control your experience. Use them with love, not pressure. Some days you'll use them often. Other days, you'll hardly need them.

The goal isn't perfection–it's connection. To yourself, to truth, and to the divine presence within.

As you shift out of ego and back into consciousness again and again, you'll begin to notice—

✦ Your thoughts are lighter.

✦ Your reactions are calmer.

✦ Your decisions are clearer.

✦ Your joy is more consistent.

You are becoming a conscious creator. One breath, one shift, one choice at a time.

"Man is made or unmade by himself."

~ James Allen

✦ Practice With Me: I Choose What Stays in My Field

Every memory, thought, or relationship holds energy.

You don't have to carry them all. You have the power to choose what stays—and what gently leaves.

✦ *Take a breath.*

✦ *Feel your body.*

✦ *Recognize that you don't have to get rid of anything.*

✦ *You're choosing to no longer keep it inside your sacred space.*

Say~

✦ *"I return to center."*

✦ *"I release all that no longer belongs in my field."*

✦ *"I choose what aligns with clarity, peace, and love."*

✦ *Imagine your space becoming lighter.*

You are using a tool that protects your energy with grace.

Chapter 16

Your Spiritual Gifts and How to Use Them

"The intuitive mind is a sacred gift, the rational mind is a faithful servant. We have created a society

that honors the servant and has forgotten the gift."

~ Albert Einstein

Every one of us possesses spiritual gifts that await us—stay open to your new discoveries. Discovering and using all your spiritual gifts is a major confidence booster. These gifts help cleanse your environment for protection and empower you.

Your Third Eye

The third eye is within the sixth chakra and is the portal to your spiritual awareness and higher consciousness. Located in the center of your forehead, often associated with the pineal gland, this small but powerful energy field is a gateway to spiritual enlightenment.

When you focus on opening and balancing your third eye throughout the day, you expand your awareness and strengthen your intuitive energy. When this center is activated, it can also be used to cleanse heavier energy.

By intentionally using awareness, you allow more energy to flow through —releasing tension and radiating light into your environment.

Whenever you sense heavy or unsettled energy from a person or place, softly open your third eye and allow light to flow through it. Let it cleanse your aura and the energy around you, restoring balance and calm.

This center can become a powerful tool for you—one that supports spiritual clarity and energetic release. With practice, when you bring your attention here, you can more easily feel the energy and presence of your third eye.

Your 3rd Energy Center Door

Your third energy center chakra—your solar plexus—is the powerhouse of all chakras. Located between your belly and ribs, it stores your deepest pain as well as your greatest vitality. It's the chakra that needs the most protection.

This center is especially vulnerable to negative energy. Have you ever received shocking news that felt like being punched in the stomach, or experienced a sudden wave of depression or heaviness in your solar plexus?

In these moments, your solar plexus may be absorbing negative energy, which can create blocks and lead to fatigue, illness, and even physical discomfort.

You can visualize a protective "submarine door" built into this chakra. You can keep it open when you're receiving energy through meditation or in any setting that feels safe and intentional.

Before entering crowds or other highly charged environments, gently close this door with the feeling of a firm, secure seal. This helps keep unwanted energy out and supports your sense of balance.

Over time, you'll develop a stronger energetic shield and may find you no longer need to use this visualization as often.

Other Spiritual Gifts

You may also begin to intuitively receive spiritual gifts—personal insights and abilities that are uniquely yours.

At an early point in my journey, I began visualizing a majestic hawk with a wingspan that seemed to stretch for miles—broad, steady and filled with light. I named him Elmer. He symbolized protection and strength, helping me stay balanced amid the intensity of my nursing school clinicals.

Calling on Elmer gave me a sense of grounding and safety, and reminded me I was supported by something greater than myself.

Later, I worked with someone who also felt drawn to the image of a hawk. He lived close to nature and longed for a greater sense of safety in the wilderness. When I encouraged him to invite a spiritual hawk to protect him, he embraced the practice wholeheartedly.

"My hawk's name is Hawk," he told me with a smile. From that day forward, Hawk became his companion in the wilderness—a living symbol of God's presence, protection, and strength surrounding him.

Each person's gifts arrive uniquely, often just when they are most needed. Sometimes, these gifts take the form of a spiritual animal who watches over you and helps neutralize fear or whatever you cannot carry alone.

The key is to stay open—these gifts always arrive at the right time, when your soul is ready to receive them.

Practice Gratitude

My life has become one of gratitude—a blessing I never take for granted. There were times I thought I had everything I needed, and still felt empty. There were times I lost what I thought I couldn't live without, only to discover something deeper waiting underneath. That's when I realized joy isn't measured by surface pleasures, feel- good relationships, or fleeting moments of happiness—it's something steadier, something rooted in the soul.

Gratitude to me, is a kind of attunement —a continual return to who you are. It softens the anxiety, calms the mind, and brings you back to the present. When you live in this space more often, it naturally becomes the energy you share with others.

If you feel anxiety when you wake up, remind yourself that it can be a messenger—not a threat. Then gently shift into gratitude. Let one grateful thought replace the anxious one. Then another. Let the pattern build, moment by moment, until gratitude becomes your natural rhythm. Leave small reminders in your space if needed, such as sticky notes, symbols, or gentle prompts that ask, "What are you grateful for right now?"

Let that habit grow.

Gratitude doesn't just happen. It takes intention—just like any other new habit you want to cultivate. With time, the practice of being grateful not only soothes the mind—it heals it. It shifts your frequency, opening the way for more peace and transformation in your life.

Give Yourself Physical Healing

Your body is the foundation of your energy. When you care for it with nourishment, movement, and rest, you create the stability your spirit needs. Healing isn't only emotional or spiritual—it's physical too. A well-care for body helps your energy flow freely, making it easier to stay clear, grounded, and connect to your own inner calm.

During energy sessions, visualize a bright white pillar of translucent light flowing into areas of pain. You can heal. You can find relief, comfort, and even transformation. Healing isn't always about elimination—it's also about creating a state where your body supports your spirit and your spirit uplifts your body.

Financial Healing

Money too carries energy. When your relationship with it becomes balanced and soul-aligned, your whole being relaxes. You breathe more deeply, sleep more peacefully, and trust that life will continue to support you.

Your true prosperity begins with a calm knowing that your needs are met. When you make decisions rooted in clarity and self-respect, you invite abundance to move through you more freely—without the resistance that comes with unconscious living.

 Living within your means and making soul-aligned choices creates a sense of safety that allows peace to expand—first within your body, and then throughout your life.

Your Imagination

Neville Goddard once said, *"Imagination is God."* When used with intent, imagination becomes one of your most powerful tools.

Visualize yourself in the reality of what you desire. *Feel* the emotions you would feel if it were here now—joy, peace, satisfaction.

Close your eyes and play a 20-second reel of your ideal moment. *Feel it*. Let that emotion set your energetic frequency— like a bell ringing its clear tone. That vibration calls harmony into your life.

Just as a bell emits a tone that invites harmony or disharmony, you emit emotional frequencies into your life. When your imagination is paired with joy and presence, it becomes creation. What you feel, you attract.

✦ Practice With Me: Heal and create With Your Mind

Whatever you visualize, you energize.

What you imagine with love and presence you create.

Part 1: Physical healing visualization

✦ *Sit or lie down.*

✦ *Place your hands over the part of your body that needs support or relief.*

✦ *Close your eyes and breathe in gently and exhale slowly.*

✦ *Visualize a pillar of warm golden light entering the top of your head.*

✦ *Let it move gently through your body, clearing tension, releasing pain, renewing the cells it touches.*

✦ *Let it pool in the space beneath your hands. See that space softening, glowing– restoring itself.*

Say~

"My body receives healing light."

"I allow renewal to happen."

"I am light and healed."

Stay here for a few minutes. Allow the light to flow until you feel complete.

Part 2: Manifestation with Imagination

Bring to mind one soul aligned desire, something simple, beautiful, and meaningful to you.

✦ *What does it feel like to live inside this reality?*

✦ *What are you seeing, hearing, or doing?*

✦ *How does your body feel in this version of life?* Let it become real in your inner world.

This is your intuition pulling you forward to where you want to be.

Say~

"I create with love, not pressure."

"I allow this vision to unfold in perfect time."

This is your sacred practice. You're not demanding. You're inviting.

PART THREE

Principles in Motion

Chapter 17

Essentials and Manifestation

Love is Our Freedom as Well as Our Limitation

Love is both our freedom and our limitation.
When we love from our heart, it expands our
lives in the most beautiful and authentic ways.
When we remain entangled in relationships or
environments rooted in negativity, we
unintentionally continue to feed it.

Love becomes our limitation when we have to
choose to detach from abuse, manipulation, or
collective toxicity. This is where love defines
what we are no longer willing to accept, creating
a ripple effect of healing and clarity.

We're Wired with a Negative Bypass

We're wired with a natural bias toward
negativity; painful emotions and experiences are
often remembered more vividly than positive
ones; especially early in life. This is part of

human survival instinct. Fear triggers the brain's "fight or flight" response, and because of this wiring the mind can easily fixate on threats and past trauma rather than hope or joy.

But love is the opposite of fear. The more love we cultivate, the less fear controls us. Awareness of these patterns helps us rise above them. When you notice a negative thought, say, *"Move on,"* and watch your energy shift. That awareness is your power.

What if I Have a Real Problem?

When you feel trapped by a problem, it's like your soul is in prison—stifled, aching for freedom. The key lies not in erasing the issue, but in changing how you hold it. You can still feel the weight of the situation while choosing to reduce its emotional grip.

Visualize placing the problem and its intensity inside a bubble and watching it float away. From this distance, you are no longer inside the problem; you are the one observing it. From that calm vantage point, you can receive intuitive guidance and respond with clarity.

You are Your New High Vibration Being

Affirmations help claim your new vibration. They are not just words—they are declarations of who you are becoming. Use them like gentle anchors: *"I am healthy." "I am provided for." "I am loved." "I am free." "I am enough."*

Your anxiety doesn't need to disappear; it simply no longer controls you. You've become someone stronger, clearer, more centered. Let your affirmations affirm the reality you are choosing to create.

Be a Victor

Being victimized doesn't mean you have to stay a victim. When someone continually gaslights or drains you, **detachment becomes a sacred boundary.** True change can't be manipulated or forced—it has to rise from within.

If the energy around you, (at work, school, or even home) is toxic, allow yourself to seek something better. Choosing a healthier environment is not weakness, it's wisdom. **Becoming a victor means protecting your space and choosing peace**.

Manifestation with an Affirmation

Wanting by itself is not enough. You must ask for what you desire. Ask boldly—not from fear, but from a heart that trusts and knows it deserves goodness.

Manifestation begins in the unseen. Keep it sacred. Let your dreams unfold in the quiet of your own soul. That inner space, untouched by others' opinions or doubts, is where you claim your transformation and create your new reality.

Stay Strong in Your Holding Period

Some chapters unfold slowly. When life feels stagnant or uncertain, you're likely in a holding period. This doesn't mean failure—it's a cocooning stage. Care for your body, tend to your spirit, and listen for what's next.

If your ego rises up with fear, gently release it. Imagine floating those anxious thoughts into a bubble and reclaiming your presence. You are no longer the old self. You're standing at the edge of your new reality, just waiting for it to bloom.

Be Extra Aware of the Random Small Ways of Thinking

The ego is sneaky. A single passing thought can shift your entire vibration. Be curious. Ask: *'What was that feeling? What just changed in me?'* Track the shift back to its source.

Often, the ego slips in through what feels small—but it carries a massive emotional echo. Confront it. Release it. These small clearings create enormous freedom.

What to Do With a Pesky Thought

Step one: Recognize It.

Step two: Detach.

If it's real, it will return with clarity. If it's ego, it will disappear.

Letting go—even for one minute—is often enough to interrupt obsessive loops. Familiar pain may feel comforting, but it's an illusion. In that one-minute shift, you reclaim hours of peace.

How Energy Can Connect You with Joy

Joy isn't a grand event—it's a soft, growing hum. It's the calm that returns when you realize you're in the flow, even if everything isn't perfect. It's the quiet celebration of who you're becoming. Joy comes in waves. Let it arrive in small doses and stay open to more.

Doing the Work for Your Own Bliss

Doing the work means showing up every day with intention.

It means detaching from fear,

connecting to Source,

and believing in what you are calling in.

Flick fear away like lint.

Practice until ease becomes your default. You are not hoping—you are creating.

Doing the Work is a Vigilance

You were born knowing abundance, and then slowly taught to forget.

Your work now is to remember who you are — without the doubt that comes with the tethered soul. Even when you're tired or uncertain, you still have the tools.

Keep detaching. Keep choosing clarity.

Some limitations are real—but most are an illusion—beliefs you've absorbed that aren't yours to carry. Many times these beliefs are heavier fabrications of memories from the past.

When you're ready, you'll rise. If you're not ready yet, believe in your ability to shift at any moment. Always trust yourself and your process.

Awareness, Healing, & Empathy

As you heal, your compassion deepens. You begin to see the world through more understanding. Everyone carries pain—some of it visible, some hidden. You soften toward yourself, and as you do so, you soften toward others. Empathy becomes your strength. Awareness becomes your light.

No Rain, No Flower: You Are in Control in All Cycles

Life is cyclical. We weather through rain and bloom. In hardship, remember that you are not the circumstance—you are the soul navigating it.

Each season will eventually pass. And when it does, it makes space for something more beautiful to blossom. Keep tending to your inner garden. Growth is happening, even when you can't see it. Gratitude waters the unseen roots.

Happiness Is a Way of Being

Happiness is what you create for yourself. It's a practice—the quiet choice to choose joy, even when things feel uncertain.

It's at peace without having all the answers, and trusting that contentment is your higher calling. It's knowing who you are and knowing you are enough. From this space of inner calm, everything yu desire begins to meet you half way.

✦ Practice With Me: Manifestation is Who You Become

You are not here to get everything "right."

You are here to stay awake—to keep learning, and to walk your path with love—as a conscious creator, not a passenger.

✦

Right now, take a moment to center yourself.

✦ *Feel your feet on the floor.*

✦ *Let your breath remind you: You are centered.*

Say~

"I am a powerful being."

"I stay awake and heal now.."

Now ask yourself gently~

✦   *What small, familiar thought has been pulling me out of joy or alignment?*

✦   *Is it fear, doubt, blame, or a limitation that feels real —but is only an illusion?*

✦   *Am I willing to release it—just for* today, and replace it with something true?

✦
Say~

"I create with joy."

✦ Practice With Me: Send Love Where Fear Once Lived

Sometimes forgiveness doesn't come all at once. It comes in layers, through clarity, through grief, and through quiet moments of surrender.

This practice isn't about excusing someone's actions—it's about freeing you from the invisible energy cords that keep you tied to pain.

Think of someone who has hurt you deeply.

You don't need to rehash the details or relive the pain. Just see their face.

✦

✦ *Now take a slow conscious breath.*

✦ *And instead of replaying the wound, speak directly to their soul.* **Say~**

✦ *I bless you.*

✦ *I send you love and light. I send healing where fear once lived.*

✦ *And I release myself from carrying your energy any longer.*

You don't need to understand how forgiveness works. You just need to feel the peace that enters your body when you release resentment.

Even if you need to repeat this every day for a while, do it with presence. Let it become part of you–not just a practice, but a path to freedom.

◆

This is not about being "nice." It's about being so free that you can offer love to the places that once held your deepest pain–and still walk away in peace.

◆

Chapter 18

Move Forward With Energy

You've come so far. Every shift you've made, every layer you've released, has brought you closer to your true self. This is the moment when the work softens. Now you simply allow. Healing isn't always about effort; sometimes it's about rest, trust, and quiet faith in what's already unfolding.

It's about being kind to yourself, trusting that you can create what you desire, and often feeling as if you already have it.

At any moment, you can shift your direction. You can choose a new thought, a new habit, a new way of being. You can become who you want to be. Life can return to you a thousandfold when you embody your truth.

That is part of the awe and joy of the process.

Even as you grown, there will be moments
when your light feels dim or distant. That's part
of being human. Energy moves in cycles—
expansion and contraction, flow and stillness.

Disappointment

It's easy to feel hopeless when life feels heavy or
unclear. When you believe every fearful
thought, the mind can feel like a cage. Some
souls are more sensitive than others, and the
collective energy of the world can amplify that
sensitivity. Yet sensitivity itself is not weakness
— it's awareness. As you learn to be your own
spiritual warrior, you begin to transform that
sensitivity into strength.

There are too many people suffering quietly, but
a wave of evolved souls has come to raise the
planet's awareness. As we all lift our own
vibration individually, we contribute to the

collective healing for all. With time, love and empathy can become the new normal.

How to Be a Spiritual Warrior with Emotions and Duality

The path of the spiritual warrior is not about perfection. It's about catching the moment when ego tries to distort your truth and it's where you choose love instead.

Fearful thoughts often arise as normal reactions to life. But ego has a tendency to intensify those thoughts, distort them, and spin them into something darker. It will exaggerate your pain, whisper lies, and try to convince you they're true.

Recognizing this duality is key. When you're aware of how ego operates, you can catch it before it takes over. That's when your inner spiritual warrior steps in — helping you shift toward truth, light, and freedom.

Fear Feels Safe

Fear often feels comfortable because it's familiar. We convince ourselves that it protects us — that if we listen to our fear, we'll stay safe and avoid mistakes. But fear keeps us stuck in old patterns, reacting instead of creating. True safety doesn't stem from fear—it comes from awareness and trust with our own strength.

Awareness vs. Resistance

Resistance is what happens when we align with ego's stories— when we believe we *are* our reactions, our moods, or our circumstances. The more resistance we build, the more ego feeds us rationalizations for staying stuck.

But you are not your fears. You are not your past. You are a conscious being who can observe thoughts and detach from them. With awareness, you become the observer — free to choose a new vibration.

Claim What You Want

The moment you shift your attention from what's not working to what you truly desire— especially with generosity and giving, your reality begins to change. Don't wait to feel satisfied — generate satisfaction through your intention.

Detach from the illusion of "lack" and claim the life that was meant for you. The universe responds to the vibration of love and clarity.

✦ Practice With Me: Choosing Happiness from Within

Happiness isn't about perfection—it's about presence.

Happiness is feeling your living truth and walking with compassion, even in difficult seasons.

Say~

"I have all the power in the world to be as happy as I want to be."

You don't need to feel good all the time.

You only need to stay loving with yourself.

That is strength and spiritual mastery.

Chapter 19

Create Your Daily Ritual

When you're having a down day, it's easy to feel like your spiritual practice isn't working. You might think, I've been doing the work, staying grateful, and trying to stay connected — so why do I feel this way?

Maybe you didn't get the job, or the thing you've been hoping for hasn't shown up. Maybe you're just exhausted. These moments are part of the process. Sometimes you're in a "bridge of incidents" — the space between intention and manifestation.

But here's the secret: what you seek is already within you. Each moment a gem is waiting to be discovered. It may be hidden by fog in the moment, but it's there. Stay open to the idea that what seems like a loss or setback may actually be an opening — a gift — in disguise.

Let yourself feel. Cry if you need to. Express your frustration. Then, when you're ready, tune in. Ask for help clearly and specifically and be open to receiving insight. Your intuition will help you. You also have a guide who's close by and would love nothing more than to be your closest ally when things feel hard.

Often, your more evolved intuition will offer a new perspective. It might show you why something isn't working out, or gently redirect your focus. Sometimes it will affirm that what you're doing is right, but that the timing just isn't aligned yet.

I used to resist meditating (tuning in), when I had a difficult day. Sometimes I'd think, why bother? This won't help. But now, I know better.

Even when I expect nothing, I'm often transformed just by showing up. Not every time — but often enough to trust the process.

Dreams

Many dreams help us release, especially fear of loss. Some are tied to our everyday life, while others help bring closure to emotions stored in your consciousness. They are a tool for emotional processing and soul communication.

Intuition Is a Soul Experience

Intuition is the ability to know without logic. When you regularly tune in and receive energy, your sixth and seventh chakras — the mind and soul portals — become clearer.

The Past Is the Past — Every New Moment Is a Choice

We all struggle with past mistakes. We replay them, judge ourselves, and wish we'd done something differently. But who you were yesterday is not who you are now. Your past does not define you — what matters is the grace you offer yourself today..

When you shift your perspective and detach from the need to control life—space opens. Sometimes, when you're deeply craving something — love, support, purpose, money, validation — the most healing thing you can do is offer it to someone else. Serve others. Create with others.

What you struggle to receive often is given back to you in unexpected ways. When your focus is on love, not lack, the universe mirrors that energy back to you.

✦ Practice With Me: On the Hard Day, You're Not Alone

You don't have to feel strong all the time.

Down days don't mean you're doing it wrong. They mean you're human, and it's time to receive.

✦ *Put your hand over your heart and* ***say~***

✦ *"I'm open to support"* and *"I am never alone."* Imagine a loving presence beside you. This might be your spiritual guide, or the intuition of your higher self.

✦ *Stay open and **ask***~

✦ *What perspective will help me feel supported?*

✦ *Let an image, a feeling, rise. Don't force it, just stay open.*

Even if you hear nothing at first, your energy has shifted.

You've made space for a connection that can come now or when the time is right.

Say,~

"I am not alone."

"I am supported."

"I trust the light within me."

On the hard days, turn inward. Your guide is not far away. Your calm is always there for you, it's not gone.

It's beneath the noise—waiting for you to listen.

Chapter 20

A Gem is Waiting to be Discovered

A Gift for You–for You to Discover

Your enlightened self is the version of you that remembers your soul. It knows what you value. It knows what's right and wrong–not from dogma, but from a deep inner knowing. Enlightenment brings wisdom, compassion, and strength.

When we're disconnected, it's easy to fall into passivity. We say, "I'm just doing what everyone else is doing," or "It's not my responsibility." This kind of detachment from truth allows harm to spread.

But when you're connected to your soul, you trust what you feel inside. You no longer need external validation. You stand for love, truth, and the highest good.

Each day you wake up is a chance for a new discovery—where a hidden treasure is waiting to be found. Even when life feels ordinary, something miraculous can shift at any moment. When we least expect it, a door opens, we gain a new perception that changes everything, or a blessing finds its way to us. Stay open to the unexpected. Believe that each sunrise carries the possibility of something beautiful, new, and completely unplanned!

Religions and Spirituality

Religion is a structured form of faith. Spirituality is a way of living in light and love. Every religion holds some truth — because all paths to God are valid when they come from love. We must move beyond argument and honor one another's devotion.

Stay Open

When you stay open, you allow the universe to show you new directions. Loss, disappointment, or redirection is often a sign of alignment — not failure.

When something ends — a job, a friendship, a chapter of your life — stay curious. Trust that new growth is already beginning, even if you can't see it yet.

Know Your Soul Self

This human life is a flash compared to your eternal soul. The more you know who you truly are, the more you can live in joy. When you forget your soul, you fall into fear and limitation. When you remember it, you feel free.

Don't let past pain or outer circumstances run your life. Every moment matters. You are your own victory leader — right now!

✦ Practice With Me: Remember Who You Are

You are not your fear.

You are not what ended, what failed, or what faded.

You are an eternal soul--wise, worthy, and whole.

✦ *Close your eyes.*

✦ *Place a hand gently over your heart.*

✦*Breathe in gently and* **say inwardly~**

"I remember who I am."

"I am light. I am soul."

"I am freer than I can even fathom."

Let that remembrance rise through your body like a quiet strength.

You are safe to stay open and receive.

Whatever has fallen away has made even more space for what is more fully aligned.

www.ingramcontent.com/pod-product-compliance
Lightning Source LLC
LaVergne TN
LVHW041314080426
835513LV00008B/454